PIECED ROMAN SHADES

Turn your Favorite Quilt Patterns into Window Hangings

Terrell Sundermann

C&T PUBLISHING

Copyright © 2000 by Terrell Sundermann
Developing Editor: Beate Nellemann
Technical Editor: Lynn Koolish
Design Director: Diane Pedersen
Copyeditor: Vera Tobin
Book and Cover Design: Kristen Yenche
Illustrator: Alan McCorkle ©2000 C&T Publishing
Front Cover Photo by Tim Murphy/Foto Imagery

Attention Teachers: C&T Publishing, Inc. encourages you to use
this book as a text for teaching. Contact us at 800-284-1114 or
www.ctpub.com for more information about C&T Teachers
Program.

We take great care to ensure that the information included in
this book is accurate and presented in good faith, but no war-
ranty is provided nor results guaranteed. Since we have no control over the choice of materials or procedures used, neither the
author nor C&T Publishing, Inc. shall have any liability to any
person or entity with respect to any loss or damage caused
directly or indirectly by the information contained in this book.

Gem-Tac™ is a trademark of Beacon Chemical Company.
Jewel-It™ is a trademark of Aleene's.
Quiltgard™ is a trademark of The Craftgard Company.
Roc-lon® and Thermalsuede® are registered trademarks of
Rockland Industries, Inc.,
Scotchgard™ is a trademark of 3M Corporation.
Teflon® is a registered trademark of Teflon Industries.
Velcro® is a registered trademark of Velcro Industries.
Window Hangings® is a registered trademark of Terrell Designs.

Page 85 notes safety concerns with Roman shades. The reader
needs to be aware of the issues pointed out in this space. In the
event that the reader makes shades to sell, he/she should com-
ply with the American National Standard for Safety of Corded
Window Covering Products. This requires the placement of a
hang tag on the shade, which can only be removed by the con-
sumer. The tag that applies to the directions given in the book is
the "Cord with Cord Stop Hang Tag." A copy of the Standard
can be purchased from the Window Covering Safety Council
(WCSC) at 355 Lexington Avenue, Suite 1700, New York, NY
10017, 800-506-4653.

Library of Congress Cataloging-in-Publication Data
Sundermann, Terrell.
     Pieced Roman Shades : turn your favorite quilt patterns into
Window Hangings / Terrell Sundermann.
        p. cm.
    Includes bibliographical references (p. 112) and index.
    ISBN 1-57120-094-0 (paper trade)
    1. Window shades. 2. Quilting. I. Title.
    TT390 .S88 2000
    746.46'0434--dc21
                              99-6794
                              CIP

Published by C&T Publishing, Inc.
P.O. Box 1456
Lafayette, California 94549

Printed in Hong Kong

10 9 8 7 6 5 4 3 2 1

CONTENTS

Acknowledgement

I would like to dedicate this book, my first effort as an author, to my husband, Ned. Without him I would not have had the luxury of putting all of my experience into words and drawings. His endless support and pride in my artistic efforts are deeply appreciated.

I would like to thank the wonderful interior designers who have worked with me to produce unusual window shades: Linda Stimson of Inner Visions Interiors, Bedford, MA; Jaime Cummings, Morrison, CO; Lynn Shannon, Denver, CO; Steve Neuman of Interior Aesthetics, Denver, CO; and Maril Wilson, Denver, CO.

I have been fortunate in having several enthusiastic quilters work with me in my business. Diedre Sousa, Maria O'Connor, and Mary Ann Tidwell spent many, many hours making Window Hangings for my clients.

Foreword

I have always sewn. My grandmother taught me to mend, to embroider, and to use a sewing machine. I made awkward crewel pieces for my mother and elaborate clothes for my dolls. When I moved into my first home, I made tab curtains and then Roman shades. I loved seeing the results of my work become a functional part of my home.

I moved into my second home and made a wall hanging: my first quilting effort. It was a log cabin pattern for my bedroom that I mounted on a stretcher frame. I loved the interaction of the fabrics and geometric forms and looked around my home for another space to display my next effort. I had many large windows, all of them uncovered. Why not make Roman shades, but with the fronts pieced?

I spent many long hours happily laying out my first Window Hanging: two shades that would be mounted on the same board for a double sliding door. I chose a Churn Dash pattern and used solid fabrics in magenta, pink and turquoise. I cut the pieces out with scissors, just as I had done for my small wall hanging. Six months later, I had assembled the two tops, which measured 36" by 84" each. When I held them up, they made a gentle curve from top to bottom, like a sail displaced by the wind. My windows, obviously, were not curved. I took all of the blocks apart, properly squared them and reassembled the two fronts. This project was turning into a nightmare. But I persisted, and late one evening, I hung my masterpiece. It looked stunning and operated properly. I went to bed happy. The next morning I rushed downstairs to see the effect of the sun back-lighting my shades. As I entered the room I was awed by the glow from my stained-glass window. But as I got closer, I was aghast at my work. The sun not only lit the front fabric, but showed the seams as well. My ragged scissor cuts showed through, as did the seams that were pressed in random directions. All of the flaws were apparent. I thought of the many, many hours that I had spent laboring on these shades. My sloppiness negated the beauty of the design.

Still, I was intrigued by the concept. I got my first book on quiltmaking. I purchased a mat, a ruler, and rotary cutter. I calibrated my sewing machine for a precise $1/4$" seam. And I planned my next window. I was hooked.

I covered every window in my home. I greatly improved my piecing techniques. I took seminars on Roman shades, studied lift hardware, and modified almost every aspect of assembling the shades to best highlight my fabric art. My shades gave me enormous pleasure. They changed with the angle of view, the lighting from the room lamps, the slant of the sun. Just entering a room brought a smile to my face.

I have designed and made Window Hangings for homes across the country, and my work has been displayed in show homes and featured in magazines. Now a new phase begins with this book. I have watched the fascination that fellow quilters show when they see a Window Hanging. I want to share the techniques that I have developed so that others can display their fabric art as a functional window shade. I hope this book will guide you in learning to decorate your home with Window Hangings.

Window Hangings: FORM and FUNCTION

A Window Hanging is a combination of a wall hanging and a Roman shade. Fabrics pieced together into a quilt pattern make the front of the shade. Then you add borders and make the quilt front into a Roman shade. The concept is straightforward; you are probably wondering, "That is so simple, why didn't I think of it?" However, there are several important steps you'll need to follow in order to achieve a successful result. Laying out the quilt design is crucial. The shade needs to fold up on the design so that it looks pleasing when down as well as when raised.

Placing a wall hanging on a window adds a new dimension to displaying it on a wall. The sunlight, shining through the pattern, creates a stained glass effect. The extra thickness of fabric at the seams looks like the lead between colored pieces of glass.

Any quilt design can be used to make the front of a Window Hanging. Traditional blocks, such as Log Cabin and Five-Patch designs, make wonderful shades. Amish patterns go well in a contemporary home. For more advanced quilters, Bargello and Watercolor techniques make marvelous displays. If you can make a quilt, you can make a Window Hanging. In fact, it is faster to make your pieced front into a shade than to quilt it.

I will be describing a technique I have developed for making a Roman shade that will best display your fabric art. Your shade will work flawlessly and add to the beauty of your handiwork. The specialized hardware described on page 21 allows you to make very large shades. I have made shades as large as 12 feet by 8 feet.

Photo: Terrell Sundermann

Oriental Delight, Terrell Sundermann, 1991.
Four panels on dining room sliding doors, 36"x 86" each.

Six Important Things to Keep in Mind as You Plan, Design and Make Your Window Hanging:

◆ You start with the finished dimensions of the Window Hanging, then lay out your design moving inward from these measurements.

◆ It is important to make all portions of your Window Hanging perfectly square as displaying it on your window will accentuate any skewedness.

◆ Your seams must be a perfect $1/4$" and pressed in the same direction on every block, as they will show when the sun shines through the shade.

◆ Use 100% cotton quilting fabrics or light to medium weight decorating fabrics. Heavy decorating fabrics become unmanageable when pieced; sheers ravel and are impossible to piece.

◆ You must back your Window Hanging with a lining fabric specifically designed to block ultraviolet light or your beautiful fabrics will fade.

◆ You should take the time to make a perfect Roman shade so your fabric art will also function flawlessly as a window treatment.

Roman Shades

A Window Hanging is made as a basic Roman shade that combines simplicity and sophistication in a practical, hardworking window treatment. These classic shades draw up from the bottom by means of cords threaded through evenly spaced rings on the back. As the shade is raised, horizontal folds form, one on top of the other. When down, the shade falls flat, covering the window.

Your Window Hanging will be designed to take this accordion folding into account. Since the folds are all the same depth, we will lay out our blocks so the folds occur at the same location in each row. This might be at the bottom of each row of blocks, or in the center. We want our Window Hanging to have a pleasing design when retracted, so we will also need to consider how the front will look when it is folded up.

Front of a Window Hanging.

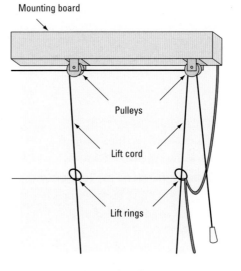

Back of a Window Hanging.

Churn Dash in Burgundy and Blue,
Terrell Sundermann, 1993.
34" x 63" and 54" x 68"

I have covered all of my own windows with Window Hangings. I have also been fortunate enough to be able to sell my creative works. Designing for other people has forced me to grow as an artist. My work has been quite diverse since my Window Hangings have been installed in all types of rooms with many different decors. The color schemes, as well as the style, are already determined, before I even begin. I very much enjoy designing within these constraints.

As you look through the photographs on the next pages, notice how the quilt patterns and fabrics fit the rooms.

Baltimore Star in Green and Pink,
Terrell Sundermann, 1993.
40" x 44"

Lone Star in Blue and Yellow,
Terrell Sundermann, 1992.
36" x 39"

Oriental Delight in Purple and Orange,
Terrell Sundermann, 1995.
29" x 72"
Interior design
by Jamie Cummings
and Lynn Shannon

Photo: Don Riely

Photo: Mark Conrad

Variations on Oriental Delight,
Terrell Sundermann, 1995.
58"x 60" center panel, 22" x 60" side panels,
12" x 29" valances.
Interior design by Jamie Cummings
and Lynn Shannon

Photo: Greg Premru

Ocean View,
Terrell Sundermann, 1996.
Four panels each 29" x 72".
Interior design by Linda Stimson,
Inner Visions Interiors

Photo : Tim Murphy / Foto Imagery

Shadows in Blue and Brown,
Terrell Sundermann, 1996.
Two panels each 68" x 66"

Oriental Delight in Blue and Pink,
Terrell Sundermann, 1996.
34" x 64"

Tumbling Star,
Terrell Sundermann, 1994.
31" x 63"

Photo: Tim Murphy / Foto Imagery

Four Diamonds in Blue and Pink,
Terrell Sundermann, 1996.
44" x 77", 42" x 77", 41" x 77",
and 43" x 77"

Four Diamonds in Blue and Pink
Terrell Sundermann, 1996.
A half-block fold Window Hanging
maximizes a beautiful view.

Photo: Tim Murphy / Foto Imagery

Illusions Valance in Blue and Purple,
Terrell Sundermann, 1997.
86" x 12"

Tumbling Bargello in Purple and Orange,
Terrell Sundermann, 1996.
97" x 58"

Photo: Tim Murphy / Foto Imagery

Illusions in Blue and Purple,
Terrell Sundermann, 1997.
87" x 94"

EVALUATING Your Windows and Rooms

Before you design your Window Hanging, you need to decide upon a quilt pattern that complements your room décor. Try to choose a small window for your first project. A Window Hanging that measures 30" to 48" wide and 48" to 60" long will sew up quickly and allow you to learn the process easily. If you don't have a small window, try and make the Shadow Window Hanging example starting on page 93.

Color on Windows

A well-planned Window Hanging combines basic design elements — color, pattern, and texture — to create a beautiful, balanced effect. No matter what quilt pattern you prefer, your initial decisions will be about color. Whether you're taking your color cues from a favorite fabric or starting from scratch, it is important to understand how color

works on your windows. In general, light colors are expansive; dark colors are more contracting. Monochromatic schemes that consist of one color in a variety of intensities and values make a room appear unified and harmonious. Light neutral colors such as white, tan, and gray are common choices for window treatments, because they put the focus on other elements in the room. If a room's scale can handle a window treatment that's bold or brightly colored, great. There's nothing like color to enliven a scheme.

Remember that you will be living with the shade for a number of years. Less-intense colors may "wear" better visually than strong ones. Repeat colors used at the windows in other places in the room to unify and balance the scheme. Take your color cues from colors you love.

Photo: Terrell Sundermann

Forest Quad, Terrell Sundermann, 1996.
Three panels, 46"x 72" each.
A single column of four diamond blocks on a cream background looks light and airy in this living room. Interior design by Jamie Cummings and Lynn Shannon

Choosing a Quilt Design

Because Window Hangings are pieced, you will create a feeling of depth on your flat shades. Using patterned fabrics adds to this depth. Although quilts are traditionally thought of as being geometrical and "country," you can create almost any effect using contemporary quilting designs and different combinations of color. A Log Cabin block in calico is definitely a country treatment. If you rotate the blocks by 45°, use jewel-toned fabrics, and highlight the blocks with light-colored background triangles, you get a contemporary look. Amish designs create a clean and modern look. Stripes and brightly colored fabrics work great in kid's rooms, bathrooms, and kitchens.

You will most likely be working with existing furnishings. Look at your room, and ask yourself the following questions:

◆ What effect do you want to achieve with your Window Hanging?

◆ Do you want it to be the center of attention?

◆ Do you want it to pull together an eclectic mix of furnishings?

◆ Do you want it to hide an old window?

◆ Which colors are already in the room?

◆ Which colors do you want to emphasize and add?

◆ Are there diamonds in the floor tiles and do you want to reproduce them in your quilt block or layout?

◆ Are the existing fabrics solids, florals, or geometrics?

The size of the quilt pattern should correspond to the scale of the room and the size of the windows. Small-scale patterns are often used in cozy rooms. Large-scale patterns should be used in spacious rooms.

The very best aid that you can make for yourself is a color board. Open up a manila folder and use the inside for your drawing. Staple or glue fabric swatches from sofas and chairs, wallpaper and carpet samples and paint chips to the other side. Take this folder with you when you look for fabrics, and keep all of your notes inside.

TIP

Ask your family about their color likes and dislikes, since they'll be living in the scheme you create.

Color board for living room.

Photo: Tim Murphy / Foto Imagery

Contemporary quilting fabrics with a feeling of texture were chosen for this breakfast nook shade.

Multiple Windows

Rooms often have more than one window. Your initial approach will probably be to cover all of the windows the same way. This may or may not work. You don't want to create the look of a quilt museum that is displaying only one quilt design. You can play with one pattern, varying it on each window, changing the scale, dropping out blocks, inserting a surprise. Combining different patterns that share at least one color or design also works well. One shade may have a pattern with all the colors in a scheme; another may contain just one hue plus white, while a third uses of two of the colors. To keep a room from looking too busy, use visually restful solids or large background areas in your shades. If you are making Window Hangings for adjoining rooms you can use the same quilt block but vary the fabrics, using one common fabric in both rooms. Or you can use some of the same fabrics, but vary the design.

One approach that works very well is to completely piece one shade that is the primary focus in the room. Then use the same block in either a single row at the top or a single column down the center on the remaining windows. This ties the windows together, but opens the room up and adds interest. Using a valance with a smaller scale block ties in the other windows. If you are doing a Watercolor pattern, you can treat each shade as a portion of one design.

Ocean View design uses a watercolor technique to create a scene on four French doors.

Also consider how large the windows are and how often you will be lowering them. I have a guest-room with two large windows in the back of the house. I leave the shades up except when we have overnight guests. Not wanting to spend a lot of time piecing the fronts, I decided on a Top Design and pieced one row of blocks at the top, then used an interesting pine-needle fabric for the rest of the shade.

Varying the layout of a quilt block adds interest to multiple windows.

Churn Dash Top Design, Terrell Sundermann, 1996. Two panels, 68" x 64" each.

Window Hanging TERMINOLOGY

The Front of a Window Hanging

The front of a Window Hanging is like the top of a quilt. Many of our terms are identical or similar to those used for quilting.

Accent border. A narrow band of fabric that is inserted between the inner front and the borders of the Window Hanging.

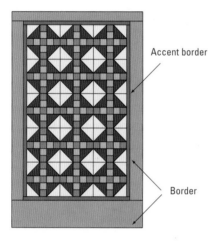

Straight set design.

Background pieces. Light-colored fabric pieces are used to highlight the pieced blocks of the inner front. These include setting triangles, corner triangles and large rectangular pieces that open up a design.

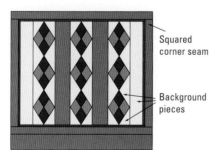

Block. The pieced fabric pattern that will be repeated on the front of the Window Hanging.

Block height. The distance that a block is repeated down the inner front of the Window Hanging. This may be simply the finished block size if a block is repeated straight, or it may be the diagonal dimension of the finished block if it is repeated on point.

Block unit. The smallest geometry of a block. Units are combined to make blocks.

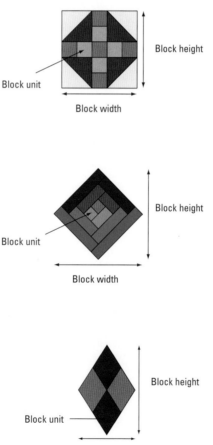

Block width. The distance that a block is repeated across the width of the inner front of the Window Hanging. This may be simply the finished block width if a block is set straight, or the diagonal dimension of the finished block if it is repeated on point.

Border. A band of fabric joined to the edges of the inner front and used to frame it.

Corner triangle. A triangle that fills in the corner of an on-point design.

Diagonal set. See On point page 20.

Floating the blocks. A block arrangement in which the corners of the outer blocks do not reach the edges of the border, making the blocks appear to float.

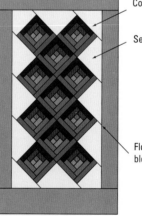

On point design.

Front. The entire side of the shade that faces the room. It includes the inner front and the borders.

Grain. The direction of the threads in a woven fabric. The lengthwise grain runs parallel to the selvage and is the most stable. A block piece or border that is cut with its longest side parallel to the lengthwise grain is cut "on-grain" and will have very little stretch. A block piece or border that is cut with its longest side perpendicular to the lengthwise grain is cut "crosswise grain" and will have more stretch.

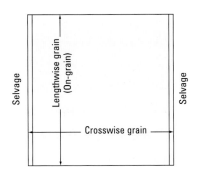

Inner front. The assembled blocks of the front. This may include sashing and background pieces.

On point. A block arrangement in which the side of the blocks run at a 45° angle to the border sides. (Also called diagonal set.)

Sashing. The fabric used to frame and separate the blocks of the inner front.

Setting triangle. A triangle used to fill in the space between blocks along the sides of an on-point design.

Squared or butted corner seam. A seam made when one border is stitched past another at a 90° angle. The seam runs parallel to the top and bottom of the Window Hanging.

Straight set. A block arrangement in which the sides of the blocks run parallel to the sides of the quilt.

The Folding of a Window Hanging

Most of our designing effort for a Window Hanging will involve taking into account the way it folds up. Read over the following terms carefully and refer to the drawings. For a hands-on demo, copy pages 25 and 26, cut out and fold.

Bottom border. The border at the bottom of the Window Hanging.

Down fold. A fold in the Window Hanging that hangs down when the shade is raised. A down fold does not have lift rings.

Finished width. The width of a Window Hanging refers to the horizontal dimension. The finished width is the width of the completed Window Hanging.

Finished length. The length of a Window Hanging refers to the vertical dimension. The finished length is the length of the completed Window Hanging.

Fold depth. The length of the folds when the shade is raised.

Full-block fold. A Window Hanging that is designed to fold up on the full block. When fully raised, the entire top row of blocks shows.

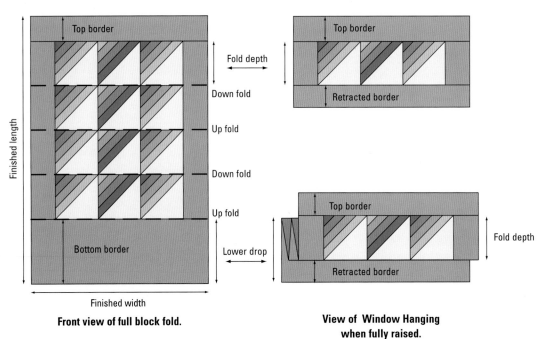

Front view of full block fold.

View of Window Hanging when fully raised.

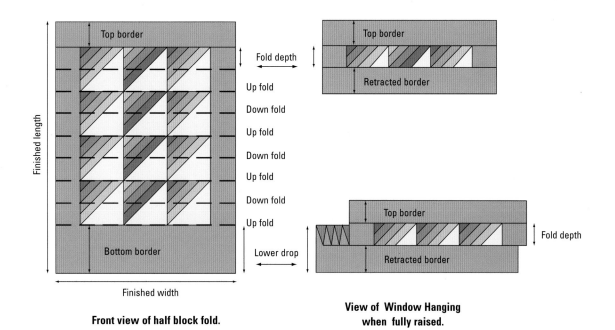

Front view of half block fold.

View of Window Hanging when fully raised.

Half-block fold. A Window Hanging that is designed to fold up on the half block. When fully raised, only the top half of the block shows.

Lower drop. The distance from the lowest row of lift rings to the bottom of the shade.

Retracted border. The portion of the bottom border that shows when the Window Hanging is fully raised. The retracted border is always equal to the lower drop minus the fold depth.

Side border. The borders at the sides of the Window Hanging. The side borders are usually designed to be of equal width.

Top border. The border at the top of the Window Hanging.

Up fold. A fold in the Window Hanging that pulls up when the shade is raised. An up fold has lift rings.

Hardware for a Window Hanging

Roman shade hardware is simple. You build it yourself, which also makes it inexpensive compared to purchasing drapery rods and finials.

1x2 board. A board, typically pine, used to mount the Window Hanging to the wall or window trim. It is nominally 1" by 2", but due to milling loss, the actual measurements are usually smaller.

Batten. A plastic or a wooden stiffener glued along each fold in a Window Hanging so that the shade folds cleanly when raised. See also Roman shade rib, page 22.

Cord drop. A plastic or wooden accessory through which lift cords are threaded. This provides an easy way to raise a shade.

Flat installation. Attaching the mounting board on the wall or window trim so that the smallest dimension of the board projects, allowing the Window Hanging to lie as flat as possible against the window.

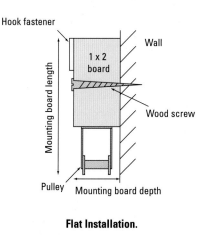

Flat Installation.

Hook and loop fastener. The tape used to attach a Window Hanging to the mounting board, commonly known as Velcro®. The hook portion is stapled onto the board, while the soft loop portion is sewn onto the top of the Window Hanging.

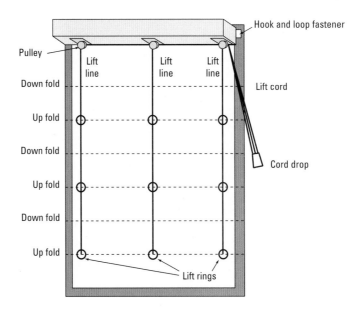

Back view of a Window Hanging.

Lift cord. Thin braided polyester cord used to lift the Window Hanging.

Lift line. A vertical column of lift rings through which the lift cord will be strung during final assembly of the Window Hanging.

Lift rings. Small plastic rings sewn in columns on the back of the shade at the up folds. Lift cords threaded through these rings cause the shade to fold up in an accordion-style.

Mounting board. The entire mounting hardware to which the Window Hanging is attached. It is comprised of a wooden board, hook fastener, and pulleys through which the lift cords are strung to raise and lower the shade.

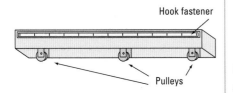

Mounting board.

Mounting board depth. The distance that the mounting board projects out from the wall or window trim.

Mounting board length. The vertical dimension of the mounting board.

Projected installation. Mounting the mounting board on the wall or window trim so the widest dimension of the board projects.

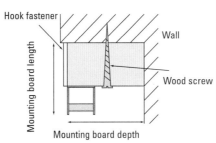

Projected installation.

Pulley. A simple wheel and axle assembly in a housing that is attached to the mounting board. The lift cords are threaded through the wheel, which allows easy lifting of the Window Hanging.

Return. The depth from the front of a valance to the wall.

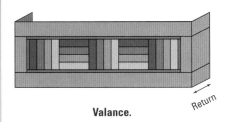

Valance.

Roman shade rib. A hollow 3/16" flexible plastic batten that is glued between the Window Hanging front and lining along each fold line, so that the shade folds cleanly when raised. This is available in 5-foot pieces and can be easily cut to any length. A 3/16" wooden batten can be used for smaller shades of up to 48" wide instead of the plastic ribs.

Roman shade rib splint. A small metal rod used to join two Roman shade ribs for making shades wider than 5 feet.

Roman shade rib.

How A Window Hanging FOLDS UP

A Roman shade folds up in an accordion-style. It is important to understand how this happens and how your Window Hanging will be designed to accommodate this folding. When the Window Hanging is folded, there are up folds and down folds. You will always have an equal number of up folds and down folds. The up folds have a row of rings sewn on the back of the shade, while the down folds don't have rings. The first (lowest) row of rings is placed well above the bottom of the shade (the lower drop). When the shade is raised, a portion of the lower drop folds up behind the shade. It is important that the lift rings are positioned correctly, otherwise a portion of the fabric front will be exposed to the sun when raised.

Why must there be an equal number of up and down folds? When you raise a Roman shade up one fold, the fabric automatically creates a down fold. If you design a Window Hanging with an unequal number of up and down folds, the top row of blocks will fold in the middle and the shade will look quite strange when fully raised. Usually the top border pooches out as well.

Half-Block Fold

You will want your shade to fold up either on the half-block or on the full-block. When the shade is folded on the half-block, the bottom of the block is always an up fold, while the middle of the block is always a down fold. When fully raised, only the top half of the block shows.

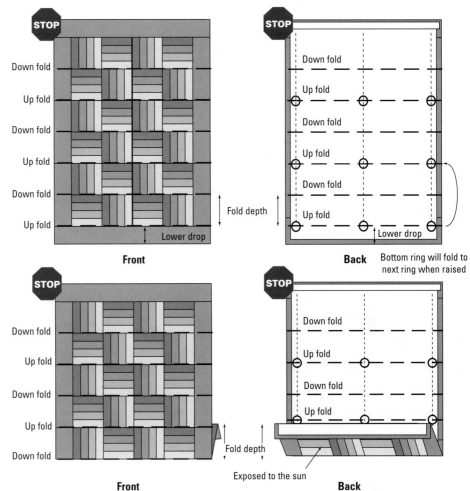

Front

Back

Bottom ring will fold to next ring when raised

Front

Back

Exposed to the sun

If the lift rings are not positioned correctly a portion of the front will be exposed to the sun when raised.

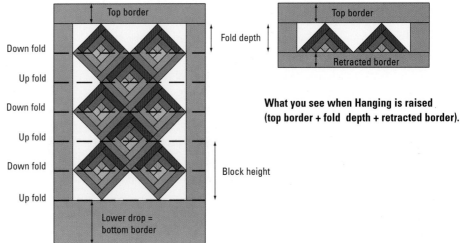

What you see when Hanging is raised (top border + fold depth + retracted border).

Remember lower drop must be larger than fold depth.

Full-Block Fold

When the shade is folded on the full-block, both the up folds and the down folds are at the bottom of the block. That is, the bottom of a row of blocks might be on either an up fold or a down fold. Since you need an equal number of up folds and down folds, you have to be concerned with the number of rows.

Full-Block Fold with Even Number of Rows

When you have an even number of rows of blocks, the first (lowest) row of rings is placed at the bottom of the lowest row of blocks. This creates the first up fold. The bottom of the next row of blocks is a down fold. When fully raised, the entire top row of blocks shows.

Full-Block Fold with Odd Number of Rows

When you have an odd number of rows of blocks and are folding on the full-block, you have to modify the position of the lowest lift rings. If they are placed at the bottom of the first (lowest) row of blocks, you will not have an equal number of up and down folds. You must therefore place the lowest lift rings at the bottom of the second row of blocks. When fully raised, the entire top row of blocks shows.

How to Choose Fold Type:

1. The length of the shade when fully raised. If you need a small length of the shade when fully raised (to maximize light into a room or maintain a beautiful view), you will find it easier to use a half-block fold layout. To get a small length of the shade when fully raised with a full-block fold, you must use a small block size.

2. The appearance of the fully retracted shade. If you want the entire block to show when the shade is pulled up, you must fold on the full-block.

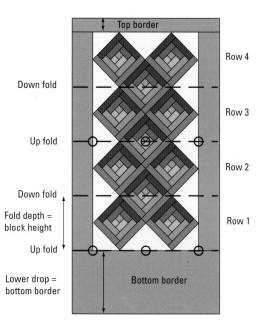

Full-block fold, EVEN number of rows.

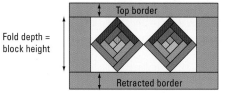

What you see when Window Hanging is raised (top border + fold depth + retracted border).

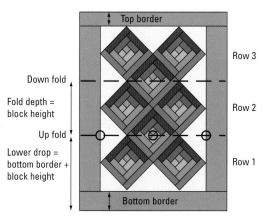

Full-block fold, ODD number of rows.

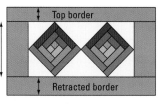

What you see when Window Hanging is raised (top border + fold depth + retracted border).

Full-Block Fold Cut-out SAMPLE

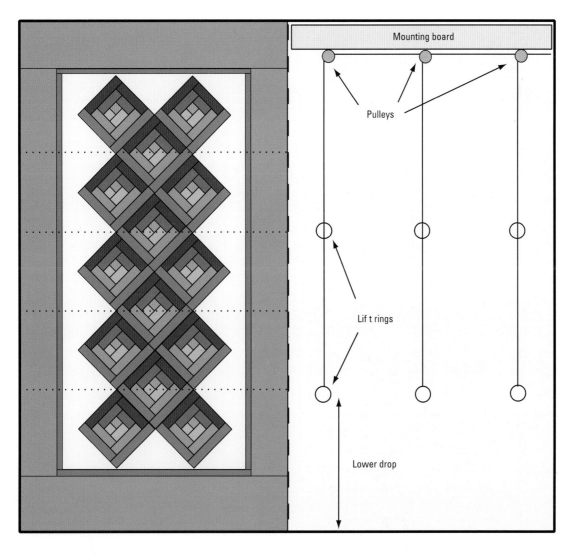

Model of a Full-block Fold Window Hanging

1. Make a copy of the page.

2. Cut out the entire front and back on the heavy black lines.

3. Fold along the dashed line. You now have the front and the back of your shade. When you turn your shade around you will see where the lift rings are in relation to the blocks.

4. With the front of the Window Hanging facing you, fold the bottom of the Window Hanging up along the lowest dotted line. Continue folding the Window Hanging in accordion fashion. (Looking at the back, the rings are at the top of each fold.) The highest fold is at the bottom of the top row of blocks. This is how your shade will look when fully raised.

5. Looking at the back, notice that the lowest row of rings folds up to meet he second row of rings. This is how your shade works when you pull the lift cords. If you look at the front of your Window Hanging you will notice that you have folded the design on the full block.

Half-Block Fold Cut-out SAMPLE

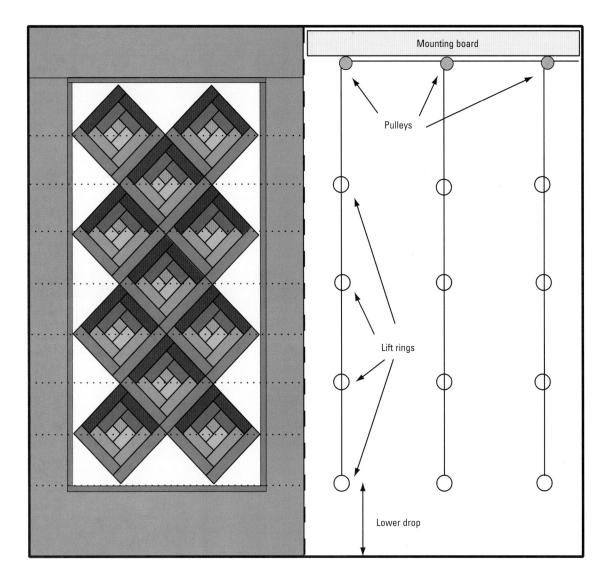

Model of a Half-block Fold Window Hanging

1. Make a copy of the page.

2. Cut out the entire front and back on the heavy black lines.

3. Fold along the dashed line. You now have the front and the back of your shade. When you turn the shade around you will see where the lift rings are in relation to the blocks.

4. With the front of the Window Hanging facing you, fold the bottom of the Window Hanging up

along the lowest dotted line. Continue folding the Window Hanging in accordion fashion. (Looking at the back, the rings are at the top of each fold.) The highest fold is at the middle of the top row of blocks. This is how your shade will look when fully raised.

5. Looking at the back, notice that the lowest row of rings folds up to meet the second row of rings. This is how your shade works when you pull the lift cords. If you look at the front of your Window Hanging you will notice that you have folded the design on the half block.

How to MOUNT a Window Hanging

Windows are designed to admit light and air and to allow views of the outside world. But windows and their treatments play a myriad of other roles, ranging from purely decorative to hardworking. Window Hangings will help you control light, provide protection from a harsh sun, keep out the cold, and provide privacy. A Window Hanging has an insulating effect. The space between the fabric and the window — a dead-air space — prevents air currents, cold or hot, from circulating.

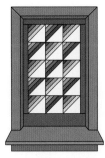

An inside mount shade fits firmly inside the top of the window frame.

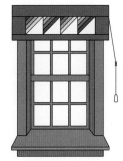

An outside mount shade is installed on the wall above the window frame.

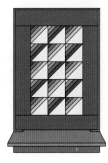

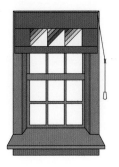

Hybrid mount.

A hybrid-mount shade is a combination mount that is placed on the window trim.

There may be multiple windows in one window frame. You need to decide if you will make separate shades or one large shade.

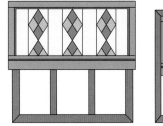

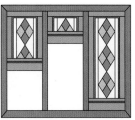

Outside mount.   **Inside mount.**

Measuring Your Window

Follow these guidelines for accurate measuring:

◆ Study your window. A trimmed window has a wood frame and may have a sill and an apron. An untrimmed window is simply recessed into the wall and has no projecting sill or apron.

◆ Sketch out the window you will be measuring, including the trim and distances to the ceiling, floor, and any other objects, such as light switches.

◆ Measure in three dimensions. You need to know not only the width and length measurements, but also the depth of the window trim and the window frame.

◆ Use a metal tape for measuring, as cloth tapes may stretch or sag. Measure to the nearest $1/8$".

◆ If you will be covering more than one window, measure every window. They will often be different sizes even though they appear identical.

◆ Take pictures.

Inside Mount

Installing a Window Hanging inside the window trim results in the cleanest look. If the window is framed in wood, the appearance is that of a picture frame around your fabric art. The shade is out of the way, even when lowered. The disadvantage of an inside mount is that you will lose part of your view and light even when the shade is fully raised. The raised shade will cover the top of your glass.

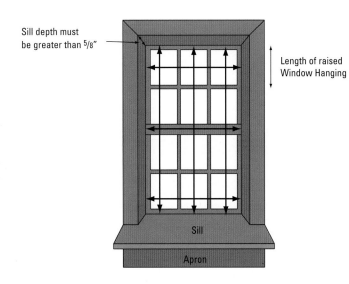

Inside mount Window Hanging dimensions:
finished width = smallest inside width less $1/4$"
finished length = smallest inside length less $1/4$".

- ◆ Measure the width and length of the inside of the window in at least three places (top, middle, and bottom).

- ◆ Measure the depth of the inside of the window frame at the top of the window where the mounting board will go. This dimension must be at least $5/8$" so that the mounting board can be placed inside the window. If it is not at least $5/8$" you cannot use an inside mount.

- ◆ Subtract $1/4$" from the smallest width and length measurements so your shade will raise and lower without rubbing the window trim.

Outside Mount

Installing a Window Hanging outside the window trim allows you to raise the shade up to the top of the glass (assuming that you have adequate wall

space between the top of the window and the ceiling) letting the maximum amount of light into the room. The sides of the shade usually extend at least 2" beyond the window trim. Otherwise there will be a gap of light that can be seen when you stand beside the window. Make sure that there is enough room around the window to allow for this over-sizing. Although these directions will give you a desired finished width and finished length of your shade, you can often vary these dimensions slightly with an outside mount, which will make laying out your design easier. The disadvantage of an outside mount is that the Window Hanging will be larger, requiring more fabric and sewing time. It is also harder to handle a large shade during construction.

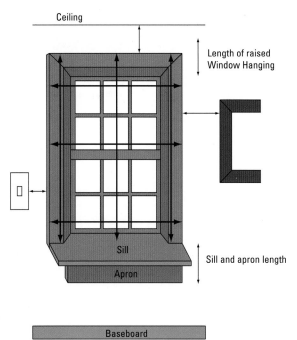

Outside mount Window Hanging dimensions:
finished width = largest trim-to-trim width + 4"
finished length = largest top trim-to-sill length + 4 $1/2$".

- ◆ Measure the width of the window from the outside of the trim in at least three places (top, middle, and bottom).

- ◆ Measure the length of the window from the outside of the top trim to the sill in at least three places (left, middle, and right).

- ◆ Survey the window and surrounding wall spaces to identify all obstacles. Measure the distance to light switches, the end of the wall, etc.

TIP

A sliding door requires an outside mount so that the shade raises above the door, allowing you to walk through it.

◆ Measure the distance from the top of the window frame to the ceiling. If the window is trimmed, this distance must be at least 4 $1/2$" so that the mounting board can be placed above the projecting trim.

Note that the Window Hanging finished length given on page 28 results in a shade that drops to the windowsill when lowered. If you want the shade to cover the lower sill and apron, or if your window is simply trimmed without a sill, use a length measurement that will cover the entire bottom trim by at least 1". Be sure to start your measurement at least 4 $1/2$" above the top trim. Measure the depth (projection) of all trim pieces as well.

Hybrid Mount

There will be situations when you will want to use a hybrid mount, where the mounting board is attached to the window trim, but not inside the window. If you want to see part of your trim, but want to maximize your view, use a hybrid mount.

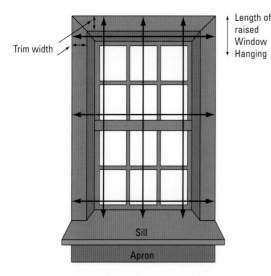

**Hybrid mount Window Hanging dimensions:
finished width = largest width
finished length = largest length.**

◆ Measure the width of the window from the outside of the trim in at least three places (top, middle, and bottom).

◆ Measure the length of the window from the outside of the top trim to the sill in at least three places (left, middle, and right).

◆ Measure the width of the window trim. Check both sides and the top. They should be the same width, but you may find they are not.

Cord Pull Position

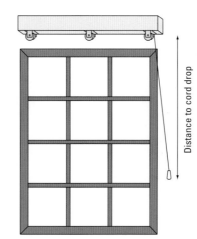

Indicate location of cord and cord drop.

On the drawing of your window, sketch where you want the cord to be. Generally it is on the right-hand side, but consider which side of the window is easiest to access. Be sure to note on your drawing where you want the bottom of the cord to end when the Window Hanging is down. A good rule is to extend your arm horizontally and touch the side of the window. This is where the cord drop should hang.

TIP

Mounting a Window Hanging on a French door is a hybrid mount, since the door functions as the window trim.

TIP

If you have small children and want to prevent them from reaching the cord, raise your arm comfortably and have the cord end there.

TOOLS and Techniques

Designing and constructing a Window Hanging involves four distinct parts:

◆ Designing the front

◆ Sewing the front

◆ Making the shade

◆ Making the mounting board

Those of you who are already experienced quilters should have the necessary tools and understand the basic techniques that will be used to make the front of a Window Hanging. If you have never made a quilt or a pieced wall hanging, read one of the basic quilting books listed in the Resources section on page 110.

Making the front of a Window Hanging into a Roman shade is a very simple process. You sew the pieced front to the lining along the side seams, making a tube, and then close the top using loop fastener. This is much faster than quilting a wall hanging. Anyone who can cut a small piece of wood and use a screwdriver can make the mounting board. Once your tools and supplies are assembled, it should take you less than half an hour to make the mounting board.

TIP

If you are using plywood to make a padded work surface, place an old blanket on your table before laying the wood on top.

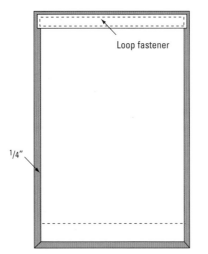

Loop fastener

1/4"

A Window Hanging is made like a pillowcase with a 1/4" turnaround of the front fabric to the back.

The Workspace Set-Up

You can use any desk area to design your Window Hanging. Natural lighting is needed to evaluate your fabric and color samples.

Space to Cut and Sew

You can use your normal sewing area when you make the front of your Window Hanging. If you do not already have a padded working surface, I strongly recommend that you make one. The padding prevents your fabric from slipping and assures that you square up your shade accurately. A surface that is 5 feet (60") by 8 feet (96") is ideal. Although you may be making Window Hangings larger than this, you can do most projects on a table this size. I now have a table this size, but began by using a padded 3/4"-thick plywood board (which is 4' x 8') that I laid on a dining room table. A design board made by covering lightweight foam core board with felt or batting that is hung on the wall is a wonderful help when you are piecing your front.

To Pad a Work Surface

Drape batting (at least 1/2" thick) on a table or 3/4" plywood board. The batting should extend around the edge and over to the back by at least 1-inch. Staple or tape on the back surface. Cover this batting with a piece of muslin, which should be slightly bigger than the batting. Begin at the center of one side and staple the muslin to the undersurface. Move to the opposite side and staple the center, stretching the muslin tightly. Repeat for the other two sides. Now staple the muslin at 2" intervals, folding the corner fabric smoothly.

Space to Make the Shade

During the final stages of making your shade, you will need a surface that is several inches larger than your finished dimensions. If this is larger than your sewing table, a good option is to use the floor. The best floor surface is a low-nap carpet. Second best is a wood, tile, or linoleum floor.

Be sure to carefully vacuum the floor before laying your fabric on it. Also, remove your shoes and work in your stocking feet. The area needs to be closed off from children and pets while the glue used to attach battens is dries. If you saw in your sewing room, be sure to spread newspaper under your work area to catch the wood and metal dust.

You will be sewing plastic rings onto the shade. Your stitches will go completely through the lining to the front of the shade. You can lay the shade on a table to do this. It is very helpful to hang the shade and work from both sides. One way to accomplish this is to staple hook fastener to the side of a ceiling beam. You can then attach the top of the shade to the beam and easily sew on the rings. You will have to stand on a chair to reach the top row of rings.

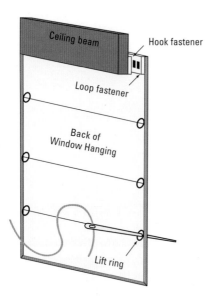

Staple hook fastener to a ceiling beam to allow access to both sides of the Window Hanging while sewing on the lift rings.

Tools and Supplies for the Front

You'll Need:

Calculator	Plastic mat
Graph paper	Ruler
Steel tape measure	Shears
16" x 24" carpenter's square	Seam ripper
48" and 72" aluminum rulers	Steam iron
#2 pencil	Plastic spray bottle
Charcoal pencil	Walking foot or
Disappearing ink marker	Teflon® presser foot
Rotary cutter	

Space to Make the Mounting Board

Making the mounting board involves sawing wood and metal. A table in a garage or workshop with a vise works great.

Planning Tools

When you design your Window Hanging, you will use copies of the forms given in the Appendix from page 102, and you might need a calculator. You will be sketching your design on graph paper. Use 1/4"-grid paper so that 1" equals 1-foot.

Measuring Tools

A steel tape measure, 12-foot or longer with a spring-return, assures easy, accurate measuring of windows and can be used to measure fabric also. A carpenter's square, available at hardware stores, is essential for squaring your Window Hanging. A 16" by 24" square is better than a smaller one. Long aluminum rulers can also be found in hardware, home supply, and art and drafting stores. I use both a 48" and a 72" aluminum ruler when squaring and measuring the Hanging during construction. You'll need fabric markers to mark cutting lines and hems. Depending upon the step, you will need a #2 lead pencil, a charcoal pencil and disappearing ink markers.

TIP

It is easier to work with two large 24" x 36" cutting mats. You will be butting these mats up against each other and also sliding them under sections of your Window Hanging to trim and square. Be sure to remove the mats before you press.

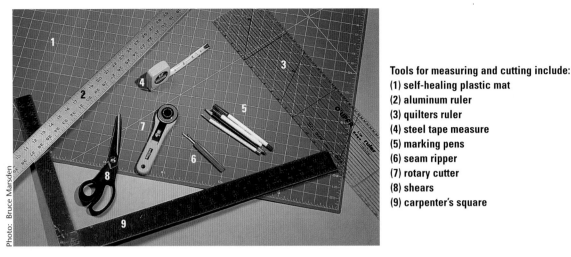

Tools for measuring and cutting include:
(1) self-healing plastic mat
(2) aluminum ruler
(3) quilters ruler
(4) steel tape measure
(5) marking pens
(6) seam ripper
(7) rotary cutter
(8) shears
(9) carpenter's square

Cutting Tools

A rotary cutter should be used to cut the fabric strips and pieces for your blocks. It is used along the edge of a cutting guide or ruler for straight cuts and done on a self-healing plastic mat to protect both the cutting surface and the blade.

A good pair of shears is useful when making initial cuts before actually trimming with the rotary cutter. A seam ripper speeds correcting any sewing errors and will be used to slit the lining hem to insert a weight rod.

Ironing Tools

A steam iron will be used at each step of your sewing. I also use a plastic spray bottle to mist the seams thoroughly. Since you'll need a larger surface than most ironing boards offer, you will find it easier to press directly on your padded table. You will need an ironing board to press the shade just after you sew the side seams in the shade.

Sewing Tools

All sewing can be done using a straight stitch on a standard sewing machine. You should have an accurate seam gauge or use masking tape to mark $1/4"$ and $3/4"$ seam locations. A Teflon presser foot or a walking foot is useful when you are attaching the lining to the pieced front. You can sew most of the seams using a neutral color thread such as gray. Use a small stitch size (10-12 stitches to an inch). You need thread that matches your border fabric to sew the hem and attach the loop fastener.

Supplies for the Roman Shade

To make a Window Hanging you need specialized hardware for Roman shades. Shops that carry shade and drapery supplies sell these items, as do some general hardware and fabric stores. A list of suppliers is listed in the Resources section, page 110.

You'll Need:	
Plastic lift rings	Jewel-It™ or
Carpet and button thread	Gem-Tac™ glue
Large eyed needle	Weight rod
Lift cord	1 x 2 board
Pulleys	Screws
Cord drop	Hook and loop
Cord cleat	fastener
Battens or Roman shade ribs	

Using specialized hardware assures that your Window Hanging will operate flawlessly.

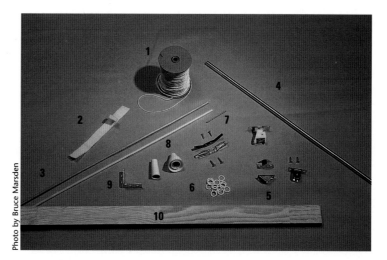

Supplies used to make a
Window Hanging include:
(1) lift cord
(2) hook and loop fastener,
(3) wood and plastic battens
   with a metal splint
(4) weight rod
(5) pulleys
(6) lift rings
(7) cord cleats
(8) cord drops
(9) angle iron
(10) 1x2 mounting board

Photo by Bruce Marsden

To Rig the Shade

To rig the shade, you need lift rings, lift cord and pulleys. The best sew-on rings are made from plastic that will not become brittle or break from sun exposure. These come in sizes from 1/2" to 3/4" outer diameter. Use carpet and button thread that matches the front of the shade and a large-eyed needle to attach the rings. The lift cord should be made from a polyester fiber that resists sunlight and that is braided to minimize stretch. Cord diameter varies from less than 1 mm to around 2 mm.

Pulleys

The lift cords are fed through pulleys to allow easy lifting of the shade. You can easily lift amazingly large shades if you use pulleys. Purchase the simplest variety you can find. You do not need swivel mounts, although these may be the only pulleys that you can find. If so, go ahead and use them. It is also not necessary to use a cord-locking pulley on the outside lift cord. I have found that any cord lock, no matter how expensive, needs replacement after about a year's use. I much prefer to wrap the cord around a cord cleat.

Cord Drop

You can finish your cords off by simply tying them together, but a nice look is to use a cord drop. These are available in several sizes. You should pick

which hang nicely and are better made than the unweighted variety.

Cord Cleat

You will need a cord cleat, which is fastened to the wall using two screws. These come in plastic (clear and smoky) and in several metallic finishes (gold, antique brass, and chrome).

Be sure you get a cleat that has two screw holes. The ones with only one screw attachment have a tendency to twirl themselves right out of the wall when you wrap the lift cord around them.

Battens

There are two items that really affect the way your shade appears when flat and how smoothly it folds up and down. The first is a batten, which you place in every fold. You can use 3/16" wooden dowels, which come in 36" and 48" lengths and are available in hardware and home supply store. A 3/16" plastic batten, called a Roman shade rib, is available in 60" lengths. The plastic battens are not only more flexible than the wood ones, but are hollow and can be extended to any length using a metal splint to join pieces. These may be hard to find, but the Resources chapter on page 110 lists a mail-order source and the wholesale supplier. You can cut both the wooden and plastic battens to any size with wire cutters.

TIP

I use a 1.8 mm cord for shades with 2 to 3 lift cords and a 1.4 mm cord for shades with more cords.

TIP

If you live in a humid climate, don't use wooden dowels, as they will warp.

TIP

My general rule is that I use steel weight rods for any shade that is under 48" wide. Shades over 48" wide are much easier to lift when you use the lighter-weight aluminum rods. Wooden dowels aren't heavy enough to effectively drop the shade.

Whether you use wooden or plastic battens, you will be gluing them to the inside of the shade using glue designed to attach hard objects, such as rhinestones to cloth. This glue, marketed under the names of Jewel-It and Gem-Tac, is available in most hobby and craft stores. Do not use regular white glue.

Weight Rod

The second item that makes your shade work well is a weight rod that you will insert into the hem of the lining. A good hardware store will carry both steel and aluminum rods. Try to get a clean-surface rod and not welding steel. If you do use welding steel, you will have to make a cloth sleeve to cover the rod before inserting it into the hem. I use both $3/8$" steel and $3/8$" aluminum rods. The aluminum is more expensive, but weighs half of what the steel does.

Mounting Board

As you are measuring your window, you should consider how you will attach the mounting board to the wall or window and on which side the lift cords will be located. You will be mounting your shade on a 1x2 board. The most readily available 1x2 is common pine. Its actual measurements are $3/4$" by $1 1/2$".

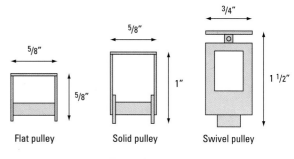

Types of pulleys.

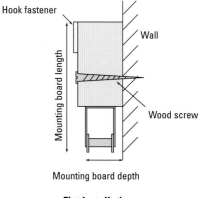

Flat Installation.

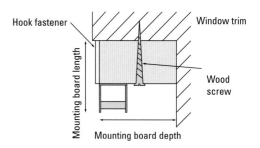

Projected Installation.

You can place the mounting board at the window in either a flat installation or a projected installation. Generally, if you are doing an outside or hybrid mount, you will be using a flat installation. This allows the Window Hanging to drop close to the window. If you are doing an inside mount, you will probably be using a projected installation and attaching the board to the top surface of the window well.

TIP

My favorite mounting board is fingerjoint pine 1x2 screen stock, which measures $11/16$" x $1 3/4$". It is very straight and the store will generally cut it to any length you want.

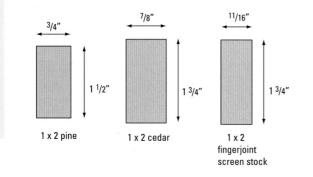

Dimensions of 1x2 boards.

You must also think about the type of pulley you use. Combining the board and the pulley gives you the mounting board dimensions. Both the depth (how far it projects from the wall) and the length (how far it hangs down) of the mounting board are important.

You will cover the board with fabric, which can either be remnants from the border fabric or lightweight white cloth. You can glue or staple the fabric onto the board. You will need screws or angle irons to install the mounting board on your window.

Hook and Loop Fastener

You will be attaching your Window Hanging to the mounting board using hook and loop fastener. Buy the softest 3/4" or 5/8" wide sew-on tape you can find. Velcro markets a soft variety that is more expensive than the normal type but is much easier to work with and gives a nicer finished look to the shade. The loop portion will be sewn onto the top of the shade using your sewing machine and matching thread. The hook portion is stapled to the mounting board.

Tools

You'll Need:	
Screw driver	Hacksaw
Staple gun and staples	C-clamps or a vise
Small hammer	Sandpaper
Wire cutters	Metal file
Hand saw	Ice pick or awl

The tools that you will need to make your shade and mounting board are a screwdriver, a staple gun and staples (1/4"), and a small hammer. You will need wire cutters to cut the battens. A hand saw and hacksaw are used to cut the wood mounting board and the weight rod, respectively. Use c-clamps or a vise to hold them in place while cutting. You should use a small piece of sandpaper and a metal file to smooth off the edges after you cut. An ice pick or an awl is useful for inserting the cords into the cord drop.

TIP

If you must skimp on hardware due to costs, use screw eyes instead of pulleys and knot the end of your pull cords instead of using a cord drop. You can even use the thicker hook and loop fastener, although you must be very careful when you sew the top closure. Do not substitute an inexpensive drapery lining or muslin for the Thermalsuede backing. Your fabrics will fade.

Tools used to make a Window Hanging include:
(1) screwdriver
(2) hacksaw
(3) ice pick
(4) hammer
(5) wire cutters
(6) c-clamps
(7) staple gun and staples
(8) sand paper and metal file
(9) hand saw

Photo by Bruce Marsden

TIP

Do not pre-wash your fabrics, which removes the sizing and dulls the colors. You will never be washing your Window Hanging.

TIP

I usually add 4" to 9" of yardage for each fabric, for those inevitable goofs.

There are three Window Hanging projects and one valance project in this book. The projects walk you through the measuring step and the layout steps, and give details on sewing the blocks. Once you have assembled the blocks, you will need to follow the instructions starting on page 57 to finish assembling the Window Hanging and to mount it.

The Appendix contains an actual example with numbers for the first Window Hanging project. You may want to read through the project and then use your calculator to reproduce the numbers in the Appendix for a thorough understanding of how a Window Hanging is designed and made.

The designs are given in order of difficulty. However, the most important thing that you can do with your first Window Hanging is to start with a small window. If you don't have any small windows that you want to cover, consider doing the example exactly as given in the Appendix on page 93. You will finish with a 30" by 47 $1/2$" sample shade that you can refer to when you make your other Window Hangings.

Determining Yardage for the Inner Front

For the projects in this book, use the Fabric Requirements Chart that is included for each project. When you are designing your own project, you will need to count the number of blocks and determine how you will piece them. Be sure to add a $1/4$" seam allowance to all edges of all pieces. Look at your border fabric layout to see if you can cut some of your block pieces from the leftover fabric. Calculate the required yardage for each fabric.

Use the same fabrics that you typically use when making a quilt – 100% cottons, blends, or chintz. You don't have to use heavy decorator-type fabrics; in fact they may be too heavy to work with comfortably. As you sew your fabric pieces together, your Window Hanging front becomes more and more substantial. Don't use sheer fabrics because they ravel too much.

Project 1: SHADOWS Window Hanging

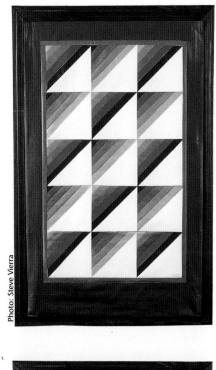

Photo: Steve Vierra

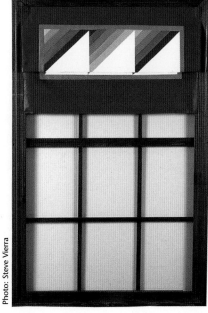

Photo: Steve Vierra

The Shadows Window Hanging is made with an Amish block. Five fabrics are sewn together in strips and then cut into triangles. Joining each striped triangle to a light-colored triangle completes the block. Since you will be cutting the strips using a rotary cutter and mat, it is most practical to vary the strip width by 1/8" increments when figuring out the block size. You can use either the full-block fold or half-block layout. See page 93 for a complete example of this project. Read all the way through the project instructions so you can gather all the needed fabric and hardware information.

TIP

You can make a sample shade by following instructions in the Appendix page 93.

1. Measure Your Window and Determine Size of Window Hanging

Review your mounting options and determine how you will mount your Window Hanging. Measure and sketch your window as described on pages 27-29, making sure to include all key measurements. Use your sketch in the Appendix on page 105 to determine the overall finished length and width of your Window Hanging.

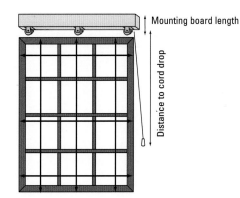

Mounting board length

Distance to cord drop

Measure your window in three places both horizontally and vertically.

2. Plan the Layout

Look at the block size chart on page 38 to see how the finished block size changes when you use strip widths that vary from 3/4" to 2".

Follow the step-by-step instructions beginning on page 60 to design the vertical and horizontal layouts. Using copies of the forms in the Appendix, pages 102-104 you will plan your block size as well as your borders.

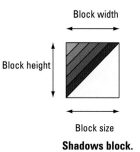

Shadows block.

3. Sketch Your Final Drawing

Use the information described on page 57 to sketch your final layout. Be sure to include the batten locations and label each fold either up or down. Your first (lowest) fold must be an up fold and your last (highest) fold must be a down fold. Also note the lift lines and lift rings (on each up fold). Sketch your block, its finished dimensions, and the number of blocks required for your Window Hanging.

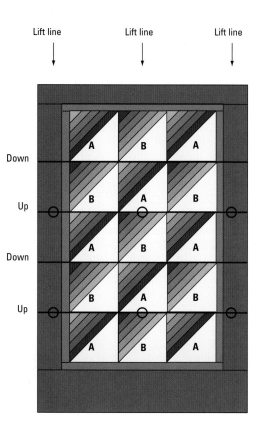

Sketch of Window Hanging with batten locations and up and down folds.

Shadows Block Size Chart

Finished Block Size	Finished Strip Size	Cut Strip Size
5 $^{1}/_{8}$"	$^{3}/_{4}$"	1 $^{1}/_{4}$"
6"	$^{7}/_{8}$"	1 $^{3}/_{8}$"
6 $^{7}/_{8}$"	1"	1 $^{1}/_{2}$"
7 $^{3}/_{4}$"	1 $^{1}/_{8}$"	1 $^{5}/_{8}$"
8 $^{5}/_{8}$"	1 $^{1}/_{4}$"	1 $^{3}/_{4}$"
9 $^{1}/_{2}$"	1 $^{3}/_{8}$"	1 $^{7}/_{8}$"
10 $^{3}/_{8}$"	1 $^{1}/_{2}$"	2"
11 $^{1}/_{4}$"	1 $^{5}/_{8}$"	2 $^{1}/_{8}$"
12 $^{1}/_{4}$"	1 $^{3}/_{4}$"	2 $^{1}/_{4}$"
13"	1 $^{7}/_{8}$"	2 $^{3}/_{8}$"
14"	2"	2 $^{1}/_{2}$"

Sketch of raised Window Hanging with a full-block fold.

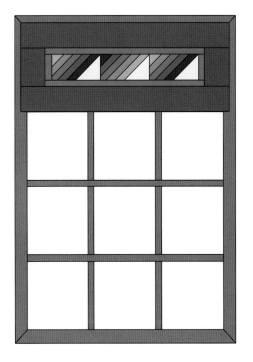

Sketch of raised Window Hanging with a half-block fold.

4. Determine Your Fabric Requirements

The Shadows blocks are made with six fabrics: five (Fabrics *a* - *e*) for the diagonal stripe pattern and the sixth (Fabric *f*) for the light-colored fabric triangle. Because of the way the striped triangle is cut, the blocks alternate with fabric *a* next to the light triangle (Shadows block A) and then fabric *e* next to the light triangle (Shadows block B). This pattern looks very nice when made with solid fabrics. You can use one color, for example, going from dark blue to light blue; or you can use multiple colors, such as blue, green, yellow and purple. Do keep the background triangle light; otherwise it distracts the eye from the striped design. If you use print fabrics, stick with tone-on-tones.

If you have not already done so, label the blocks in your drawing, starting with A and then B. The top row will be A B A B A . . . . The second row will be B A B A B . . . . Continue alternating blocks until you have filled in all rows. Count the number of A blocks and the number of B blocks and note this on your drawing.

Use the Fabric Requirements Charts to determine how much yardage you need of each of the six fabrics for your chosen block size.

TIP

Make sure you allow extra fabric for blocks for mistakes and extra fabric for borders to compensate for block inaccuracies.

Fabric Requirements for Colored Strip Sets
Fabrics *a - e*

Finished Block Size	Size of Cut Strip	Number of blocks you can make from 1/4 yard of each fabric	Number of blocks you can make from 1 strip of fabric
5 1/8"	1 1/4"	28 A blocks and 28 B blocks	8
6"	1 3/8"	18 A blocks and 18 B blocks	6
6 7/8"	1 1/2"	18 A blocks and 18 B blocks	6
7 3/4"	1 5/8"	10 A blocks and 10 B blocks	4
8 5/8"	1 3/4"	10 A blocks and 10 B blocks	4
9 1/2"	1 7/8"	8 A blocks and 8 B blocks	4
10 3/8"	2"	8 A blocks and 8 B blocks	4
11 1/4"	2 1/8"	4 A blocks and 4 B blocks	2
12 1/4"	2 1/4"	4 A blocks and 4 B blocks	2
13"	2 3/8"	3 A blocks and 3 B blocks	2
14"	2 1/2"	3 A blocks and 3 B blocks	2

How to use fabric requirements charts:

(a). Highlight the line in the chart for your chosen block size.

(b). Refer to your diagram to see how many blocks you need.

(c). Find the number of blocks that can be made from 1/4 yard of fabric.

(d). Divide the number of blocks you need by the number of blocks that can be made from 1/4 yard to determine how many 1/4 yards of fabric you will need. If this number is a fraction, round up to the next whole number.

Example: If you need eight A and seven B 13" blocks (using the larger of A and B requirements):

8 (blocks needed) divided by 3 (blocks per 1/4 yard) equals 2.7. Round this up to 3. So you need 3 x 1/4 yard or 3/4 yard of each color.

Fabric Requirements for Solid Triangles
Fabric f

Finished Block Size	Cut Size of Block for Half Square Triangle	Number of Triangles you can get from 1/2 yd of fabric	Number of Blocks that can be cut from 1 strip of fabric
5 1/8"	6"	36	12
6"	6 7/8"	20	10
6 7/8"	7 3/4"	20	10
7 3/4"	8 5/8"	16	8
8 5/8"	9 1/2"	8	8
9 1/2"	10 3/8"	6	6
10 3/8"	11 1/4"	6	6
11 1/4"	12 1/8"	6	6
12 1/4"	13 1/8"	6	6
13"	13 7/8"	4	4
14"	14 7/8	4	4

How to use fabric requirements charts:

(a). Highlight the line in the chart for your chosen block size.

(b). Refer to your diagram to see how many triangles you need.

(c). Find the number of triangles that can be made from 1/2 yd of fabric.

(d). Divide the number of triangles you need by the number of triangles than can be made from 1/2 yard, to determine how many 1/2 yards of fabric you will need. If this number is a fraction, round up to the next whole number.

Example: If you are using 8 A and 7 B 13" blocks:

15 (triangles needed) divided by 4 (triangles per 1/2 yard) equals 3.75. Round this up to 4, so you need 4/2 or 2 yards of fabric for the triangles.

5. Determine Your Border Fabric Requirements

Use the instructions given on page 69 to determine your border fabric requirements. I often use a solid fabric. Follow the directions on page 71 to sketch your border and accent border fabric layouts, marking all dimensions clearly.

You will need these drawings when you shop for fabric and when you assemble your shade.

6. Determine Your Lining Requirements

Follow the directions starting on page 71 to determine the amount of lining needed and to sketch a cutting diagram.

7. Determine Your Hardware Requirements

Make a copy of the Hardware Shopping List in the Appendix and fill it out (as described starting on page 106) for your specific Window Hanging.

Important things to remember during your construction process.

◆ Measure and cut your block pieces and strips as carefully as possible.

◆ Press seams in the same direction for every block.

◆ Whenever possible, press the seams toward the darker fabric.

◆ Square up each block to the same size.

◆ At each step you should measure, measure, measure. Don't wait until you have a fully assembled front to get out that tape measure.

8. Sew the Shadow blocks

Cut and sew stripes

Use the Fabric Requirements for Colored Strip Sets table to determine the size of the cut strip for fabrics *a* though *e* for your block size, and to determine how many strips you need to cut. For example, a finished block size of 7 3/4" has cut strips of 1 5/8". Using a rotary cutter and mat, cut fabrics *a* through **e** crosswise into the appropriate width strips. Sew the strips together in groups of five: fabric **a**, fabric **b**, fabric **c**, fabric **d**, fabric **e**. Press seams in one direction.

Cut triangles

Use the instructions below to make a template for cutting the triangles. Using the template, mark triangles along the entire length of each pieced strip set. Cut triangles. Using the template, mark and cut the required number of solid triangles from fabric **f**.

Template Chart

Finished block size	Triangle height (h)
5 1/8"	4 1/4"
6 "	4 7/8"
6 7/8"	5 1/2"
7 3/4"	6 1/8"
8 5/8"	6 3/4"
9 1/2"	7 3/8"
10 3/8"	8"
11 1/4"	8 5/8"
12 1/4"	9 1/4"
13"	9 7/8"
14"	10 1/2"

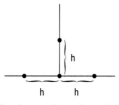

(a) Draw a base line and then draw a line that is at a right angle to the base line.

(b) Using the template chart above, mark the triangle height (h) as shown.

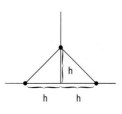

(c) Connect the points that you have marked. NOTE: This template, as drawn, already includes 1/4" seam allowances.

Use template to cut striped triangles.

Sew the solid triangles to your striped triangles and press seam towards the pieced section. Place your blocks on your design board or work surface in the order indicated in your Window Hanging sketch. Make sure that you alternate A blocks with B blocks.

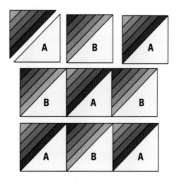

Sewing the blocks together.

9. Sew Blocks Together

Sew the inner front together by joining the blocks in each row and then seaming the rows together.

10. Complete the Window Hanging Front and Make the Shade

Use the directions starting on page 76 to cut out and attach the accent borders and borders to make your front. Make your pieced front into a Window Hanging.

Project 2: ORIENTAL Delight Window Hanging

Photo: Steve Vierra

Photo: Steve Vierra

The Log Cabin block is a wonderful choice for a Window Hanging. It is a classic design that uses fabrics and colors well. The Oriental Delight design turns the log cabin blocks on point with the dominant color down. The rotated blocks are then "framed" with light-colored setting and corner triangles. Read all the way through the project instructions so you can gather all the needed fabric and hardware information.

When working on this Window Hanging, note that when we talk about block size we are referring to the actual size of the block. When we talk about block height and width, we will be using the diagonal measurement since the block will be set on point.

1. Measure Your Window and Determine Size of Window Hanging

Review your mounting options and determine how you will mount your Window Hanging. Measure and sketch your window as described on pages 27-29, making sure to include key measurements. Use your sketch (Appendix page 105) to determine the overall finished length and width of your Window Hanging.

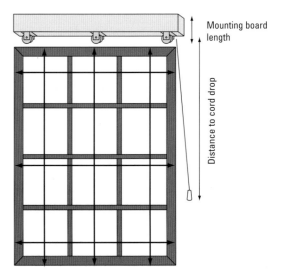

Mounting board length

Distance to cord drop

Measure your window in three places both horizontally and vertically.

2. Plan the Layout

Look at the block size chart to see how the finished block size changes when you use strip widths that vary from 3/4" to 2". Remember that this is the actual block size; however because the block is used on-point, the block height and width that you need to use in the vertical and horizontal layouts is not the same as the finished block size. Instead, you will need to use the diagonal measurement that you can find in the block size chart.

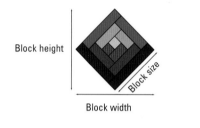

Oriental Delight block.

Follow the step-by-step instructions beginning on page 60 to design the vertical and horizontal layouts. Using copies of the forms in the Appendix starting at page 102, you will plan your block size as well as your borders.

3. Sketch Your Final Drawing

Use the information described on page 57 to sketch your final layout. Be sure to include the batten locations and label each fold either up or down. Your first (lowest) fold must be an up fold and your last (highest) fold must be a down fold. Also note the lift lines and lift rings (on each up fold). Sketch your block, its finished dimensions, and the number of blocks required for your Window Hanging. Since the blocks interlock, you need to count the blocks to arrive at the correct number. In our illustration, a layout that has two columns and three rows results in eight blocks.

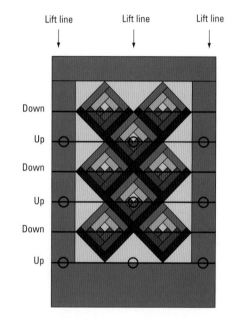

Sketch of Window Hanging with batten locations and up and down folds.

TIP

Make sure you allow extra fabric for blocks for mistakes and extra fabric for borders to compensate for block inaccuracies.

Oriental Delight Block Size Chart

Finished Block Size	Finished Strip Size	Cut Strip Size	Diagonal Size (Block Height and Width)
4 1/2"	3/4"	1 1/4"	6 3/8"
5 1/4"	7/8"	1 3/8"	7 3/8"
6"	1"	1 1/2"	8 1/2"
6 3/4"	1 1/8"	1 5/8"	9 1/2"
7 1/2"	1 1/4"	1 3/4"	10 5/8"
8 1/4"	1 3/8"	1 7/8"	11 5/8"
9"	1 1/2"	2"	12 3/4"
9 3/4"	1 5/8"	2 1/8"	13 3/4"
10 1/2"	1 3/4"	2 1/4"	14 3/4"
11 1/4"	1 7/8"	2 3/8"	15 7/8"
12"	2"	2 1/2"	16 7/8"

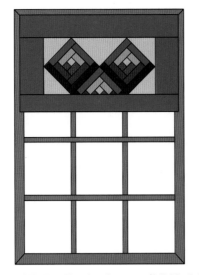

Sketch of Window Hanging drawn up (full-block fold).

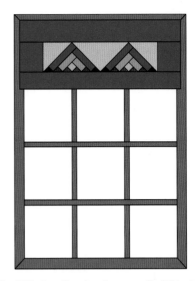

Sketch of Window Hanging drawn up (half-block fold).

Fabric requirements for Oriental Delight Blocks

Finished Block Size	Cut Strip Size	[⋯ Number of blocks you can make from 1/8 yard of fabric ⋯]					
		color a	color b	color c	color d	color e	color f
4 1/2"	1 1/4"	96	24	15	36	18	12
5 1/4"	1 3/8"	87	21	12	33	15	9
6"	1 1/2"	78	18	12	30	15	9
6 3/4"	1 5/8"	48	12	6	18	8	4
7 1/2"	1 3/4"	44	10	6	16	8	4
8 1/4"	1 7/8"	42	10	4	14	6	4
9"	2"	40	8	4	14	6	4
9 3/4"	2 1/8"	36	8	4	12	6	4
10 1/2"	2 1/4"	34	8	4	12	6	2
11 1/4"	2 3/8"	16	3	2	6	2	1
12"	2 1/2"	16	3	2	5	2	1

How to use fabric requirements charts:

(a) Highlight the line in the chart for your chosen block size.

(b) Refer to your diagram to see how many blocks you need.

(c) Find the number of blocks that can be made from 1/8 yd of fabric.

(d) Divide the number of blocks you need by the number of blocks than can be made from 1/8 yard of fabric, to determine how many 1/8 yards of fabric you will need. If this number is a fraction, round up to the next whole number. Do this for each color.

Example: If you need eight 12" blocks:
For color ***a***: 1/8 yard is more than enough.
For color ***b***: 8 (blocks needed) divided by 3 (blocks per 1/8 yard) equals 2.66. Round this up to 3 so you need 3/8 yard.
For color ***c***: 8 divided by 2 equals 4. So you need 4/8 or 1/2 yard.

Repeat for the other colors.

4. Determine Your Fabric Requirements

Although there are many different ways to make a Log Cabin block, I like to use six fabrics: three of one color range and three of a second color range. You can use a neutral color such as cream or tan for the background triangles to create contrast and make the rotated blocks stand out. If you choose a color close to, but lighter than, the block fabrics, you will have a subtler look. The border fabric can be one of the fabrics that you used in the blocks or a complementary border fabric.

You will cut the Log Cabin pieces from strips. Use the Fabric Requirements Chart on page 44 to determine how much yardage you need of each of the six fabrics for your chosen block size.

Setting triangles

The oversized setting and corner triangles are used to "frame" the blocks (the triangles are oversized to allow for squaring and trimming the Window Hanging). The corner triangles are cut as half-square triangles and the setting triangles are cut as quarter-square triangles. For one Window Hanging, you will need to cut two of the appropriate size squares for the corner triangles and one of the appropriate size squares for every four setting triangles that you need.

Yardage requirements for setting and corner triangles

For finished block sizes of 4 $1/2$" to 6 $3/4$" you can get at least 8 setting triangles and the four corner triangles from $1/2$ yard of fabric. If you need more than 8 setting triangles, you can get at least 12 setting triangles per additional $1/2$ yard of fabric. The exact number of triangles will depend on your block size.

For finished block sizes of 7 $1/2$" to 12", you can get at least four setting triangles plus the four corner triangles from $5/8$ yard of fabric. You can get at least eight setting triangles from each additional $5/8$ yard of fabric. The exact number of triangles will depend on your block size.

5. Determine Your Border Fabric Requirements

Use the instructions given on page 69 to determine your border fabric requirements, making sure you include extra to compensate for any inaccuracies in your block sizes. Follow the directions on page 71 to sketch your border and accent border fabric layouts, marking all dimensions clearly.

6. Determine Your Lining Requirements

Follow the directions starting on page 71 to determine the amount of lining needed and to sketch a cutting diagram.

7. Determine Your Hardware Requirements

Make a copy of the Hardware Shopping List in the Appendix on page 106, and fill it out for your specific Window Hanging(s).

Important things to remember during your construction process.

◆ Measure and cut your block pieces and strips as carefully as possible.

◆ Press seams in the same direction for every block.

◆ Whenever possible press the seams toward the darker fabric.

◆ Square up each block to the same size.

◆ At each step you should measure, measure, measure. Don't wait until you have a fully assembled front to get out that tape measure.

KEY: 1–5 indicates piece position
a–f indicates colors
a, b, c light colors
d, e, f dark colors

Oriental Delight Block Cutting Chart – Light Colors

Finished Block Size	Finished Strip Width	Cut Strip Width	[Cut Strip Length]				
			1a	2b	3b	4c	5c
4 1/2"	3/4"	1 1/4"	1 1/4"	2"	2 3/4"	3 1/2"	4 1/4"
5 1/4"	7/8"	1 3/8"	1 3/8"	2 1/4"	3 1/8"	4"	4 7/8"
6"	1"	1 1/2"	1 1/2"	2 1/2"	3 1/2"	4 1/2"	5 1/2"
6 3/4"	1 1/8"	1 5/8"	1 5/8"	2 3/4"	3 7/8"	5"	6 1/8"
7 1/2"	1 1/4"	1 3/4"	1 3/4"	3"	4 1/4"	5 1/2"	6 3/4"
8 1/4"	1 3/8"	1 7/8"	1 7/8"	3 1/4"	4 5/8"	6"	7 3/8"
9"	1 1/2"	2"	2"	3 1/2"	5"	6 1/2"	8"
9 3/4"	1 5/8"	2 1/8"	2 1/8"	3 3/4"	5 3/8"	7"	8 5/8"
10 1/2"	1 3/4"	2 1/4"	2 1/4"	4"	5 3/4"	7 1/2"	9 1/4"
11 1/4"	1 7/8"	2 3/8"	2 3/8"	4 1/4"	6 1/8"	8"	9 7/8"
12"	2"	2 1/2"	2 1/2"	4 1/2"	6 1/2"	8 1/2"	10 1/2"

8. Make the Blocks

Make the Log Cabin blocks by cutting the required number of strips for each fabric and then cutting out the individual pieces. You will need to calculate the number of strips based on the number of blocks you are making and the cut length of each strip. The cut lengths for each piece are given in the Oriental Delight Cutting Charts.

Begin by sewing the two center squares (1a and 1d) together using a 1/4" seam. Continue adding pieces as shown until you complete the block. You will always be pressing towards the most recently sewn piece.

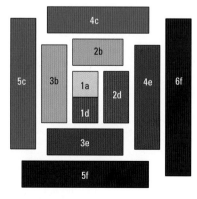

Sewing the block together.

9. Sew the Blocks Together

Cut the appropriate oversized setting triangles based on your finished block size and the number of triangles that you need. You will need to cut two squares for corner triangles.

Lay out the inner front on a work surface or a design board. Assemble the top in diagonal rows. Trim away the excess background triangle corners before attaching to the next diagonal row. Be sure to match the intersections of the log cabin blocks. Press towards the log cabin blocks, away from the light-colored background triangles. One set of seams will be "twisted" in the center to accomplish this (the seam is pressed to one side at the bottom of the piece and then reverses sides somewhere in the middle).

10. Complete the Window Hanging Front and Make the Shade

Use the directions starting on page 76 to cut out and attach the accent borders and borders to your Window Hanging. Then make your pieced front into a shade.

Oriental Delight Block Cutting Chart – Dark Colors

Finished Block Size	Finished Strip Width	Cut Strip Width	Cut strip length					
			1d	2d	3e	4e	5f	6f
4 1/2"	3/4"	1 1/4"	1 1/4"	2"	2 3/4"	3 1/2"	4 1/4"	5"
5 1/4"	7/8"	1 3/8"	1 3/8"	2 1/4"	3 1/8"	4"	4 7/8"	5 3/4"
6"	1"	1 1/2"	1 1/2"	2 1/2"	3 1/2"	4 1/2"	5 1/2"	6 1/2"
6 3/4"	1 1/8"	1 5/8"	1 5/8"	2 3/4"	3 7/8"	5"	6 1/8"	7 1/4"
7 1/2"	1 1/4"	1 3/4"	1 3/4"	3"	4 1/4"	5 1/2"	6 3/4"	8"
8 1/4"	1 3/8"	1 7/8"	1 7/8"	3 1/4"	4 5/8"	6"	7 3/8"	8 3/4"
9"	1 1/2"	2"	2"	3 1/2"	5"	6 1/2"	8"	9 1/2"
9 3/4"	1 5/8"	2 1/8"	2 1/8"	3 3/4"	5 3/8"	7"	8 5/8"	10 1/4"
10 1/2"	1 3/4"	2 1/4"	2 1/4"	4"	5 3/4"	7 1/2"	9 1/4"	11"
11 1/4"	1 7/8"	2 3/8"	2 3/8"	4 1/4"	6 1/8"	8"	9 7/8"	11 3/4"
12"	2"	2 1/2"	2 1/2"	4 1/2"	6 1/2"	8 1/2"	10 1/2"	12 1/2"

Oriental Delight Setting and Corner Triangles Cutting Chart

Finished Block Size	Size of Cut Square for Setting Triangles Yields 4 triangles per square	Size of Cut Square for Corner Triangles Yields 2 triangles per square
4 1/2"	8 1/8"	4 3/8"
5 1/4"	9 1/8"	4 7/8"
6"	10 1/4"	5 3/8"
6 3/4"	11 1/4"	5 7/8"
7 1/2"	12 3/8"	6 1/2"
8 1/4"	13 3/8"	7"
9"	14 1/2"	7 1/2"
9 3/4"	15 1/2"	8"
10 1/2"	16 1/2"	8 5/8"
11 1/4"	17 5/8"	9 1/8"
12"	18 5/8"	9 5/8"

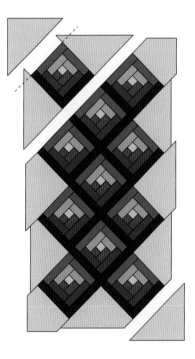

Sewing the blocks and background together.

Photo: Bruce Marsden

A rectangular block works very well with many windows. I created the Illusions design after seeing a similar pattern on bed linens. The block is made with two triangles that form a rectangle whose length is twice its width. The block is reversed at every other location, so that the completed pattern forms diamonds. You can use either a full-block or half-block layout.

1. Measure Your Window and Determine Size of Window Hanging

Review your mounting options and determine how you will mount your Window Hanging. Measure and sketch your window as described on pages 27-29, making sure to include key measurements. Use your sketch (the Appendix, page 105) to determine the overall finished length and width of your Window Hanging.

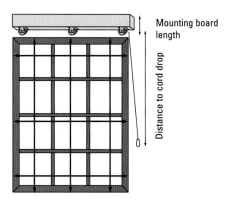

Mounting board length

Distance to cord drop

Measure your window in three places both horizontally and vertically.

Photo: Bruce Marsden

2. Plan the Layout

Look at the Illusions Block Size Chart to see how the finished block changes from 2 1/2" wide by 5" long to 6" wide by 12" long.

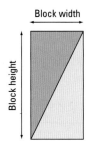

Block width

Block height

Follow the step by step instructions beginning on page 60 to design the vertical and horizontal layouts. Using copies from the Appendix, from page 102, you will plan your block size as well as your borders. Note that with the Illusions block, the block height is different from the block width.

3. Sketch Your Final Drawing

Use the information as described on page 57 to sketch your final layout. Be sure to include the batten locations and label each fold either up or down. Your first (lowest) fold must be an up fold and your last (highest) fold must be a down fold. Also note the lift lines and lift rings (on each up fold). Sketch your blocks, their finished dimensions, and the number of blocks required for your Window Hanging.

Make sure to include a sketch of how the shade will look when it's raised. Fill in an Illusions Triangle Chart from the Appendix page 108, for your design. You will use this to determine your fabric requirements. See example on page 51.

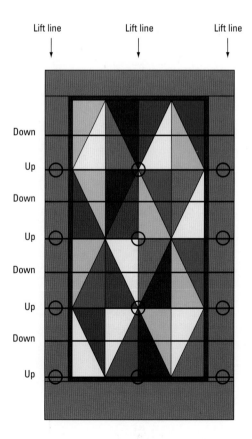

Sketch of Window Hanging with batten locations and up and down folds.

Illusions Block Size Chart

Finished Block Length	Finished Block Width	Cut Length	Cut Width	Number of Triangles per strip of fabric
5"	2 1/2"	6 3/8"	3 1/8"	24
5 1/4"	2 5/8"	6 5/8"	3 1/4"	24
5 1/2"	2 3/4"	6 7/8"	3 3/8"	22
5 3/4"	2 7/8"	7 1/8"	3 1/2"	22
6 "	3 "	7 3/8"	3 5/8"	22
6 1/4"	3 1/8"	7 5/8"	3 3/4"	20
6 1/2"	3 1/4"	7 7/8"	3 7/8"	20
6 3/4"	3 3/8"	8 1/8"	4"	20
7"	3 1/2"	8 3/8"	4 1/8"	18
7 1/4"	3 5/8"	8 5/8"	4 1/4"	18
7 1/2"	3 3/4"	8 7/8"	4 3/8"	18
7 3/4"	3 7/8"	9 1/8"	4 1/2"	16
8 "	4 "	9 3/8"	4 5/8"	16
8 1/4"	4 1/8"	9 5/8"	4 3/4"	16
8 1/2"	4 1/4"	9 7/8"	4 7/8"	16
8 3/4"	4 3/8"	10 1/8"	5"	16
9"	4 1/2"	10 3/8"	5 1/8"	14
9 1/4"	4 5/8"	10 5/8"	5 1/4"	14
9 1/2"	4 3/4"	10 7/8"	5 3/8"	14
9 3/4"	4 7/8"	11 1/8"	5 1/2"	14
10"	5"	11 3/8"	5 5/8"	14
10 1/4"	5 1/8"	11 5/8"	5 3/4"	12
10 1/2"	5 1/4"	11 7/8"	5 7/8"	12
10 3/4"	5 3/8"	12 1/8"	6 "	12
11"	5 1/2"	12 3/8"	6 1/8"	12
11 1/4"	5 5/8"	12 5/8"	6 1/4"	12
11 1/2"	5 3/4"	12 7/8"	6 3/8"	12
11 3/4"	5 7/8"	13 1/8"	6 1/2"	12
12 "	6"	13 3/8"	6 5/8"	12

TIP

Make sure you allow extra fabric for blocks for mistakes and extra fabric for borders to compensate for block inaccuracies.

TIP

Cut each rectangle individually into triangles, don't stack.

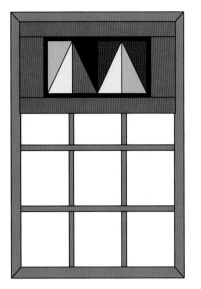

Sketch of Window Hanging drawn up (full-block fold).

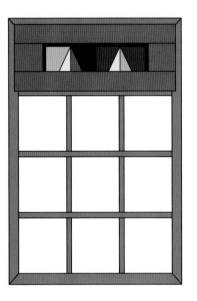

Sketch of Window Hanging drawn up (half-block fold).

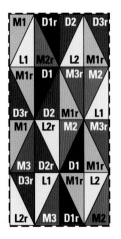

Illusions color layout (repeat as needed).

4. Determine Your Fabric Requirements

The Illusions design uses eight fabrics: two light colors, three medium colors, and three dark colors. This pattern looks very nice when made with either batik or suedes. Your color scheme might center on a multi-colored batik fabric (usually this will be a medium-colored fabric) with coordinating fabrics for the rest of the pattern. Use the drawing below to place each of your fabrics into your design. The four-row by four-column pattern can be repeated in any direction for larger shades. Repeat the pattern if necessary, then draw a red square around the number of rows and columns for your own shade*. Highlight your block size and figure your yardage for each fabric using the Fabric Requirements Chart.

*Copy and fill out an Illusions Triangle Chart (Appendix page 108) so you know how many triangles you need from each piece of fabric.

Draw a red box around your size.

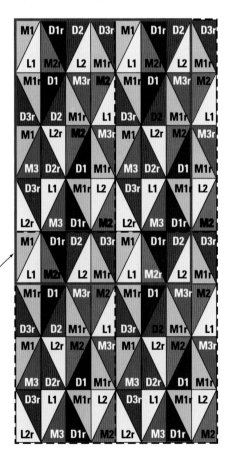

Illusions color layout.

KEY:
L = Light colored fabric
M = Medium colored fabric
D = Dark colored fabric
r = reverse triangle

Example Illusions Triangle Chart

	Number of Normal Triangles	Number of Reversed Triangles	Total Number of Triangles
Light 1	3	0	3
Light 2	2	2	4
Medium 1	2	5	7
Medium 2	3	1	4
Medium 3	2	2	4
Dark 1	2	2	4
Dark 2	2	1	3
Dark 3	0	3	3

Fabric Requirements Chart for Large Blocks

Finished Block Height	Finished Block Width	Number triangles per 1/2 yard
7 3/4"	3 7/8"	16
8 "	4"	16
8 1/4"	4 1/8"	16
8 1/2"	4 1/4"	16
8 3/4"	4 3/8"	16
9 "	4 1/2"	14
9 1/4"	4 5/8"	14
9 1/2"	4 3/4"	14
9 3/4"	4 7/8"	14
10 "	5 "	14
10 1/4"	5 1/8"	12
10 1/2"	5 1/4"	12
10 3/4"	5 3/8"	12
11"	5 1/2"	12
11 1/4"	5 5/8"	12
11 1/2"	5 3/4"	12
11 3/4"	5 7/8"	12
12"	6 "	12

Fabric Requirements Chart for Small Blocks

Finished Block Height	Finished Block Width	Number triangles per 1/4 yard
5"	2 1/2"	24
5 1/4"	2 5/8"	24
5 1/2"	2 3/4"	22
5 3/4"	2 7/8"	22
6"	3"	22
6 1/4"	3 1/8"	20
6 1/2"	3 1/4"	20
6 3/4"	3 3/8"	20
7"	3 1/2"	18
7 1/4"	3 5/8"	18
7 1/2"	3 3/4"	18

How to use fabric requirements charts:

(a) Highlight the line in the chart for your chosen block size.

(b) Refer to your diagram to see how many triangles you need.

(c) Find the number of triangles that can be made from 1/4 or 1/2 yd of fabric.

(d) Divide the number of triangles you need by the number of triangles than can be made from 1/4 or 1/2 yards to determine how many 1/4 or 1/2 yards of fabric you will need. If this number is a fraction, round up to the next whole number. Do this for each color.

Example: For color a: If you need 15 triangles for the 12" x 6" block

15 (triangles needed) divided by 12 (triangles per 1/2 yard) equals 1.25. Round this up to 2 so you need 2 x 1/2 or 1 yard.

Repeat for the other colors.

5. Determine Your Border Fabric Requirements

Use the instructions given on page 69 to determine your border fabric requirements, making sure you include extra to compensate for any inaccuracies in your block sizes. If you use an accent border, make sure the fabric contrasts well with the fabric on the side edges of the inner front. I often use a solid fabric. Follow the directions on page 71 to sketch your border and accent border fabric layouts, marking all dimensions clearly.

You will need these drawings when you shop for fabric and when you assemble your shade.

6. Determine Your Lining Requirements

Follow the directions starting on page 71 to determine the amount of lining needed and to sketch a cutting diagram.

7. Determine the Hardware Requirements

Make a copy of the Hardware Shopping List in the Appendix on page 106, and fill it out for your specific Window Hanging.

8. Make the Blocks

Cut the rectangles

See the Illusions Block Size chart to determine the cut length of your block and the number of triangels you get from 1 strip of fabric. Cut strips from each of your eight fabrics. The strip width is the cut length of your block. Now cut each strip into rectangles, using the cut width for your block size.

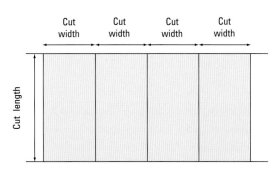

Cut fabric into strips, then cut rectangles.

Cut the triangles

Cut each rectangle into the normal and reversed triangles. Be careful when cutting the rectangles on the diagonal. Even a small error will result in your points not meeting.

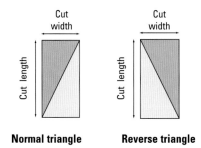

Normal triangle   **Reverse triangle**

Make a template as described below and use the template to cut off the sharp point on each triangle. Be sure to reverse the template when needed.

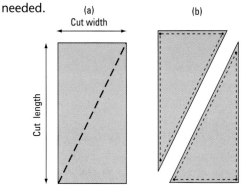

(a) Using the appropriate cut length and width for your project (see page 49) cut a rectangular template from transparent graph paper or template plastic. The 1/4" allowances are already included. Cut the template diagonally.

(b) Carefully mark 1/4" sewing lines on templates. Mark points where sewing lines meet with dots.

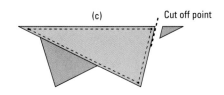

(c) Match the dots and trim off the point on the long side of one triangle.

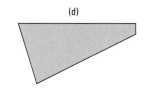

(d) Use this template to trim off the point on the long side of each fabric triangle.

Important things to remember during your construction process.

◆ Measure and cut your block pieces and strips as carefully as possible.

◆ Press seams in the same direction for every block.

◆ Whenever possible, press the seams toward the darker fabric.

◆ Square up each block to the same size.

◆ At each step you should measure, measure, measure. Don't wait until you have a fully assembled front to get out that tape measure.

Sew the blocks

Join the triangles into blocks using $1/4''$ seams. Carefully press the seams to one side, keeping the block square. Place the blocks back on your design board in the order indicated in your sketch.

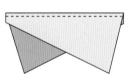

Match ends carefully.

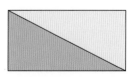

Press seams to one side.

9. Sew Blocks Together

Sew the inner front together by joining the blocks in each row and then sewing the rows together.

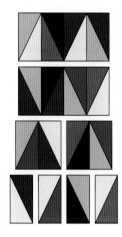

Joining the blocks together.

10. Complete the Window Hanging Front and Make the Shade

Use the directions starting on page 76 to cut out and attach the accent borders and borders to your Window Hanging. Then make your pieced front into a shade.

Project 4: Illusions VALANCE

Photo: Bruce Marsden

A window valance is a stationary "topper" that dresses the upper portion of a window. It can be used alone or over other treatments, such as wood blinds, pleated shades or curtains. Perhaps you already have perfectly functional, but uninteresting, mini-blinds. You can make a pieced valance to add your own character to the room.

The techniques we have described to design and make a Window Hanging can be used to make a window valance. Since there are no folds, the layout is simplified and there is no need for lift rings, lift cord, or pulleys. Before beginning a valance, read pages 86-89 on Making a Valance and refer to the appropriate sections as needed while working on your valance. Make a copy of the Fabric and Supplies Shopping List in the Appendix on page 107, so that you can plan your valance and make your shopping list, as you read, before you actually start on a valance. You will also need copies of the Horizontal Layout Form, in the Appendix on page 104.

Making the Illusions valance

The Illusions Block makes a wonderful valance. In the project photo, the block is turned on its side and used in two rows, making a diamond shape. If instead you are using a square block for a valance, you will probably have one row, either set straight or on point. Refer back to Project Three (pages 48-53) for instructions on determining fabric requirements and making the Illusions Block.

1. Measure Your Window and Determine Valance Mounting

Review your two mounting options and determine how you will mount your valance. Measure and sketch your window as described below making sure to include key measurements. Use your sketch to determine the overall finished length, width and depth of your valance. See page 88 for valance mounting options.

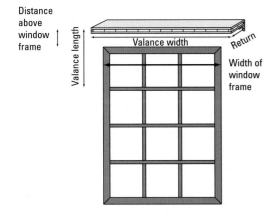

Measure the top of the window and the existing treatments in three dimensions to determine height, width, and depth.

2. Plan the Layout

Use the Illusions Triangle Chart on page 49, and the Horizontal Layout Form (page 104) to determine the block size and side borders for the valance front, ignoring the returns (if there are any, these will be added to the side border measurements.)

Determine the top and bottom borders based on the length of the valance using two rows of blocks.

3. Sketch Your Final Drawing

Draw your valance, noting block size, borders, finished width and length, and returns.

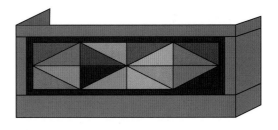

Layout of valance.

4. Determine Your Fabric Requirements

The Illusions valance is made with nine fabrics: three light colors, three medium colors, and three dark colors. The basic pattern contains two rows and eight columns. Refer to Project Three page 51 for the Fabric Requirements Chart and cutting plans. Remember that the block height and width for the valance are reversed from those for the Window Hanging, but the number of triangles that can be cut from the given amount of fabric are the same.

Fill out the Illusions Valance Triangle Chart (Appendix page 108) so you know how many triangles you will need from each fabric. See an example on page 56.

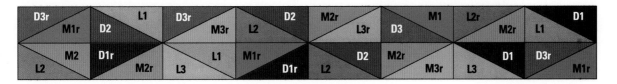

Illusions valance color layout. Repeat this pattern across your inner front.

KEY:
L = Light colored fabric
M = Medium colored fabric
D = Dark colored fabric
r = reverse triangle

Example of Illusions Valance Triangle Chart

	Number of Normal Triangles	Number of Reversed Triangles	Total
Light 1	3	0	3
Light 2	3	1	4
Light 3	2	1	3
Medium 1	1	3	4
Medium 2	1	4	5
Medium 3	0	2	2
Dark 1	2	2	4
Dark 2	3	0	3
Dark 3	1	3	4

5. Determine Your Border Fabric Requirements

Use the instructions given for valances on page 87 to determine your border fabric requirements. Remember that if your valance has returns, those measurements will get added to the borders. If you use an accent border, make sure the fabric contrasts well with the fabrics on the side edges of the inner front. I often use a solid fabric. Sketch the fabric layouts for your border and accent border (if appropriate), marking all dimensions clearly. You will need these drawings when you shop and assemble your shade.

6. Determine Your Lining Requirements

Follow the directions starting on page 88 to determine the amount of lining needed for your valance, and to sketch a cutting diagram.

7. Determine Your Hardware Requirements

Look at page 87 on making a valance. For hardware requirements you only need a board, and hook and loop fastener.

Important things to remember during your construction process.

◆ Measure and cut your block pieces and strips as carefully as possible.

◆ Press seams in the same direction for every block.

◆ Whenever possible, press the seams toward the darker fabric.

◆ Square up each block to the same size.

◆ At each step you should measure, measure, measure. Don't wait until you have a fully assembled front to get out that tape measure.

8. Make Your Valance

Follow the instructions in Project Three to make the Illusions blocks, remembering that the block height and width for the valance are reversed from those of the Window Hanging. Assemble the columns of blocks and then join the columns to make the inner front.

See pages 86-89 for directions on making a valance.

How to LAY OUT a Window Hanging

This chapter assumes you are working on a specific project. Please see page 93 in the Appendix if you would like to see a completed example.

You will start with the finished shade dimensions and then vary the block size and the border widths to design a Window Hanging that fits your window. The outside dimensions of your Window Hanging are fixed and cannot be changed, however the size of your blocks and borders can be changed to suit your needs.

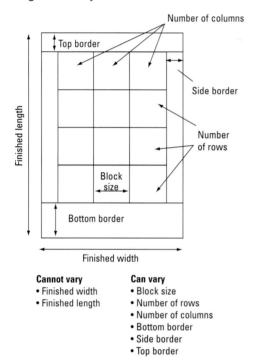

Cannot vary
• Finished width
• Finished length

Can vary
• Block size
• Number of rows
• Number of columns
• Bottom border
• Side border
• Top border

Key elements for designing the front of a Window Hanging.

In this chapter we will go through the process for laying out the front of a Window Hanging for both half-block and full-block folds.

Full-Block Folds. One important thing to keep in mind if you use full-block folds is that the number of rows of blocks in your shade is important. It affects where the lift rings are placed and how the shade is drawn up.

During the vertical layout process we will restrict ourselves to an even number of rows for full-block folds. Then in Step 4 when we adjust the top and bottom borders, we will also decide whether to add another row of blocks at the bottom of the shade. This decision will be based on how the Window Hanging looks when down. The shade will look the same when fully raised. The placement of the lift rings will be discussed in step 5.

Don't be intimidated by the layout process. If you have ever modified a quilt pattern, added sashing, or changed a border width, you have made similar calculations. We'll go through the process step-by-step using copies of the layout forms that you can find in the Appendix. You will want to make multiple copies of each one for your projects and keep the originals for future projects.

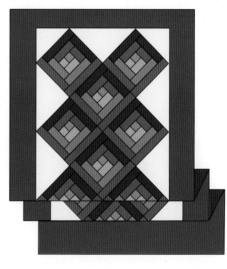

Making a scale model of your Window Hanging.

As you are working on your project, it is very helpful to draw out your design, marking where the folds are and then picturing how the shade will look when it is raised. I strongly suggest drawing your Window Hanging to scale and then cutting it out and folding it up. Any design errors are readily apparent and the extra work is well worth while.

TIP

The most important thing for you to do in the entire layout process is to draw the *vertical layout* of your shade accurately and to add up all of the block and border dimensions. These must equal your final length. Check that the bottom border meets the minimum requirements.

Step 1: Determine the Possible Block Sizes

Look at the Block Size Chart for your project. This chart shows you how your block size changes when the units that make up your block are changed by $1/8"$ (the smallest amount that is practical). It is important to note that even an $1/8"$ change to each piece of a block can have a significant impact on the final block size. For example, varying the block unit of the four-patch block by $1/8"$ results in a total block size that varies in increments of four times $1/8"$, or $1/2"$.

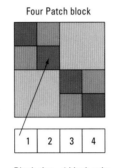

Four Patch block

Block size = 4 block units

Varying block unit in $1/8"$ increments results in block size variations of $4/8" = 1/2"$.

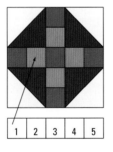

Churn Dash block

Block size = 5 block units

Varying block unit in $1/8"$ increments results in block size variations of $5/8"$.

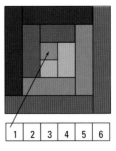

Log Cabin block

Block size = 6 block units

Varying block unit in $1/8"$ increments results in block size variations of $6/8" = 3/4"$.

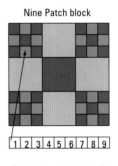

Nine Patch block

Block size = 9 block units

Varying block unit in $1/8"$ increments results in block size variations of $9/8" = 1 1/8"$.

Although it is possible to use any size block, I have found the following boundaries to produce pleasing designs:

Block unit size

This depends upon the fabric pattern. Small-scale prints translate into smaller pieces better than large-scale prints. If a fabric is really interesting, like a batik, I try to use large pieces. I personally don't like to work with finished block unit sizes smaller than $3/4"$.

Block size

5" to 12" finished blocks are okay, although I prefer 7" to 10". In general, the larger the window, the larger the block should be. If you are covering a small window in a large room, a large block also looks nice.

The following illustrates how to measure block size, height, and width.

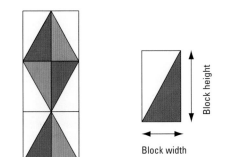

Rectangular block has different block height and block width.

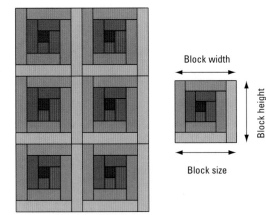

Square block stepped over inner front

Block size = block width = block height.

For those of you who like to "wing it", go ahead. Use a block size you are comfortable with, adjust the borders to fill in the required space and make the front. Before you make the shade, lay the front on a worktable, fold in the seam allowances and then fold the shade up. You may have to move the folds.

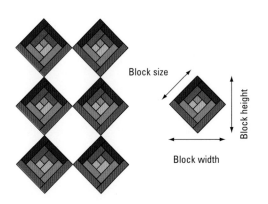

Square block stepped on point over inner front

Block width = block height = 1.41 x finished block size.

Step 2: Design the Vertical Layout

Decide upon a half block fold or a full block fold design. See How Your Window Hanging folds up on page 23.

Laying out the vertical measurements of your Window Hanging is your most important task so we will consider it first and deal with the horizontal layout second. Use a blank copy of the Vertical Layout Form to record your measurements. The form for the half block fold layout is slightly different from the form for the full block layout so be sure you are working with the proper form for your particular project. You will find the forms in the Appendix on pages 102 and 103.

a. Determine the smallest top border.

> The **First Vertical Layout Rule** is that the top border must be long enough so that it does not interfere with the lifting hardware.

If we examine the back of a Window Hanging when it is fully raised, we see that the shade can only be raised to the bottom of the pulley.

The last (highest) fold raises the lift rings to the top of the highest row of blocks. For our designing purposes, this means that the top border must be equal to or longer than the mounting board length. We must also add in the lift ring diameter.

> Smallest top border = mounting board length
> + lift ring diameter

TIP

If you have not yet purchased your mounting board and associated hardware, use a smallest top border size of 4".

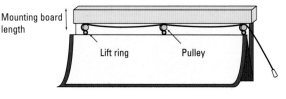

The mounting board and lift ring determine the smallest size for the top border.

b. Choose an initial finished block size.
Choose a finished block size based on the size of your window and the room. Choosing the block size at this point is a best guess process to get the layout started. You will probably need to make some changes before you finalize your design.

c. Determine the smallest bottom border.
The smallest size of the bottom border is based on your block size and whether you are using a full-block or half-block fold.

> The **Second Vertical Layout Rule** is that the the bottom border must be long enough to cover the back-facing fold completely with at least 1" extending down past the folds.
>
> If you are using a **half-block fold**:
>
> Smallest bottom border =
> $1/2$ of the block height + 1"
>
> If you are using a **full-block fold**:
>
> Smallest bottom border =
> the block height + 1"
>
> *(Note - this is for an even number of rows of blocks. If your shade turns out to have an odd number of rows, the smallest size of the bottom border is 1.")*

d. Determine the largest size of the inner front length.
(the space available for your blocks). The largest size of the inner front length is the finished length of the Window Hanging minus the smallest sizes of the top and bottom borders.

> Largest inner front length =
> finished length - smallest top border
> - smallest bottom border

e. Fill inner front with blocks.
After you have determined how much space you have for the blocks, see how many whole blocks you can fit vertically within the allotted space. If you are using the full block fold and you have an odd number of blocks, use one less block. If after you adjust your borders you decide you want an odd number of rows read the special discussion on page 67.

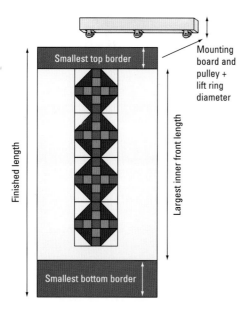

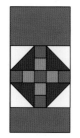

h. Picture how the shade will look when it is fully raised

Full-block fold.

f. Calculate the adjusted size of the inner front length.

(the number of rows times the block height).

g. Adjust the bottom border so that the entire inner front is filled in.

Adjusted bottom border = finished length - adjusted inner front length - top border

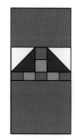

Half-block fold.

The retracted border is the portion of the border that is seen when the Window Hanging is fully raised and part of the border is hidden. For full-block folds the retracted border = bottom border minus the block height. For half-block folds the retracted border = bottom border minus half the block height.

i. Evaluate the layout and repeat the process as needed.

The first attempt at a layout will almost never be ideal. The shade may be too long when it is fully raised, or you may have too many rows of blocks. Repeat step *b* through *h* as many times as needed with different block sizes. If you are using the full-block fold, you will find that you will be trying more block sizes than with the half-block fold layout, since you are restricted to an even number of rows at this point. The length of the shade when raised will jump around as you change the block size. Try smaller blocks as well as larger blocks to come up with a pleasing layout.

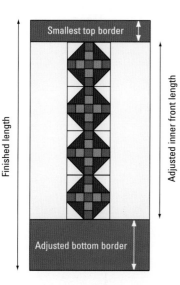

What Happens When You Decrease the Block Size?

The following illustrates what happens when you decrease the block size.

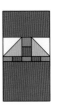

What you see when the Window Hanging is fully raised.

STEP 1: Choosing the initial block size and setting the bottom border.

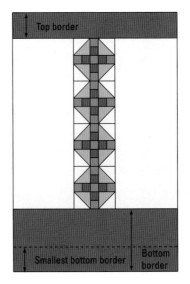

What you see when the Window Hanging is fully raised.

STEP 3: Making the block size smaller yet results in an even larger bottom border. More of the Window Hanging will show when fully raised.

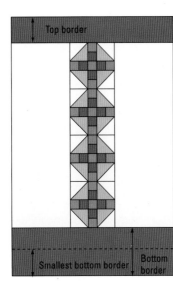

What you see when the Window Hanging is fully raised.

STEP 2: Making the block size smaller results in a larger bottom border. More of the Window Hanging will show when fully raised

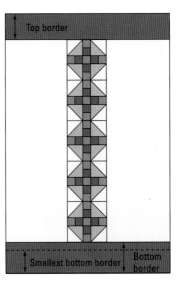

What you see when the Window Hanging is fully raised.

STEP 4: Making the block size small enough to add another row finally results in a smaller bottom border. The length of the fully raised Window Hanging is reduced, but you will need to sew an extra row of blocks.

What Happens When you Increase the Block Size?

You can reduce the length of the raised shade more easily by increasing the block size than by decreasing it.

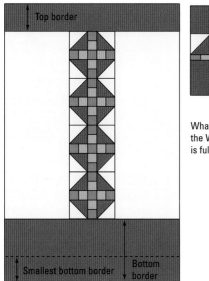

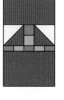

What you see when the Window Hanging is fully raised.

STEP 1: Choosing the initial block size and setting the bottom border.

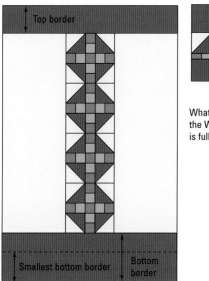

What you see when the Window Hanging is fully raised.

STEP 2: Making the block size larger results in a smaller bottom border. Less of the Window Hanging will show when fully raised.

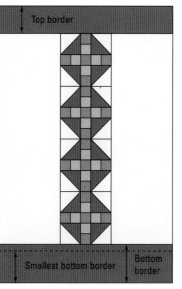

What you see when the Window Hanging is fully raised

STEP 3: Making the block size even larger results in an even smaller bottom border. Less of the Window Hanging will show when fully raised.

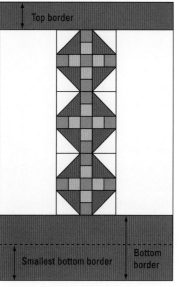

What you see when the Window Hanging is fully raised

STEP 4: Making the block size still larger requires elimination of a row. More of the Window Hanging will show when fully raised.

Now that you understand what is happening as you change the block size, you can use the appropriate Vertical Layout Form in the Appendix to lay out the vertical dimension of your Window Hanging. Make several copies of the form. Be sure to sketch out your final layout. Enter the final values for the top and bottom border lengths and the block height. Add the numbers together and confirm that you have the correct finished length.

Step 3: Plan the Horizontal Layout

Laying out the horizontal dimension of your Window Hanging is simple. There are no rules that constrain the width of the side borders. The side borders will be dictated by the finished width and the width of the block that was used to plan the vertical layout. Also, the side border width will be the same on the left side and the right side. The sum of the block widths and the two side borders must equal the finished width.

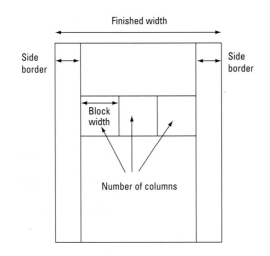

Key elements for designing the horizontal layout.

The block width is determined by the block size we used for our final vertical layout, so we will vary the number of blocks across and the side borders. I generally start with a side border of 4", and see how many blocks will fit across the inner front width. There is no problem overlapping the side borders, since you can widen or narrow them to fit.

The horizontal layout process is

a. Use your final vertical layout drawing to determine your block height and width.

b. Choose an initial side border (generally from 2" to 7").

c. Determine the initial inner front width (which is the finished width minus the two side borders).

d. Place as many blocks as possible across the inner front width.

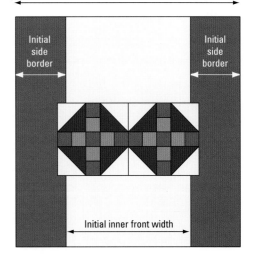

e. Determine adjusted inner front width. (Number of blocks across x block width).

f. Widen or narrow the side borders to fill the entire front.

g. If necessary, add or subtract columns of blocks and adjust the side borders to fit.

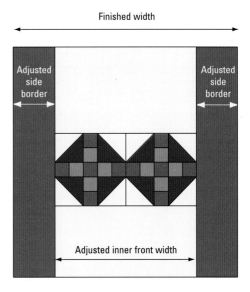

Don't be afraid to use wide side borders. They usually look better than narrow borders. Use a copy of the Horizontal Layout Form in the Appendix page 104 to work through the horizontal layout for your Window Hanging. Sketch your final layout and enter the final values for the side borders and the block width. Add up these numbers and confirm that you match the correct finished width.

Step 4: Adjust the Borders

Our next step is to adjust the top and bottom borders to obtain a pleasing design. During the vertical layout process, you set the top border to the smallest value allowed by your mounting board. You may want to increase that top border.

At this point, the inner length is fixed. (It is equal to the block height times the number of rows.) Since the finished length is also fixed, we can think of sliding the inner front width up and down to get an optimum "frame" around our quilt design. But remember our two Vertical Layout Rules (see page 60). We cannot go higher than the smallest top border or lower than the smallest bottom border, or our shade will not pull up correctly.

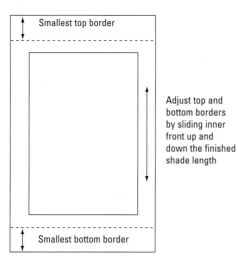

Adjusting the top and bottom borders.

The easiest way to adjust the top and bottom borders is to use the total border length, which is now also fixed:

Total border length = top border + bottom border

You can use any combination of top and bottom borders that adds up to the total border length, as long as they are each larger than their smallest values as set by the Vertical Layout Rules. You also need to be sure to calculate the retracted border (bottom border less the block height) and verify that it is larger than 1".

I like to think of the Window Hanging as a matted picture. Generally the top and sides of a mat are equal, while the bottom is larger. This gives weight to the picture. With our restrictions on our top and bottom border lengths, we cannot always achieve this, but I try to get close. Keep testing values until you have numbers that please you.

If you are using full-block folds and your bottom border is very long, you should try adding a row of blocks at the bottom of the shade, resulting in an odd number of rows. Follow the procedure at the end of this chapter, starting on page 67. When doing this:

◆ Adjust the numbers in your vertical layout drawing and make sure that all the rules are met.

◆ Keep in mind that you will usually want the bottom border to be at least as large as the top border.

Step 5: Your Final Design

You should now sketch a picture of your shade to scale, label the fold lines with "up" and "down," and then draw the shade when it is fully raised. (See page 23 if you need a refresher on up and down folds). Put all of the information from the Vertical and Horizontal Layout Forms on your drawing. Be sure to include any border adjustments that you made. You will be using this sketch to calculate yardage and hardware requirements and during the construction process. You can leave out the block details, or roughly sketch in several blocks. If you decide to sketch the block details, you can color the drawing using colored pencils so that you can visualize your Window Hanging. If you are making more than one shade, draw each one and place them next to each other to see the effect of your multiple designs.

Placing the Lift Lines

Decide where your lift lines will be located. You will have a lift line 1" in from each edge and additional columns of rings approximately 12" to 20" apart across the width of the shade. It is easiest to place the lift lines at the edges or centers of the blocks. They do not have to be evenly spaced.

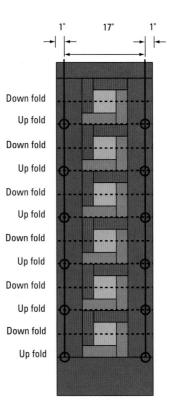

Lift lines at outside edges.

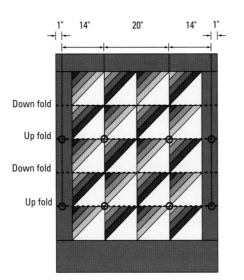

Lift lines placed at edges of block.

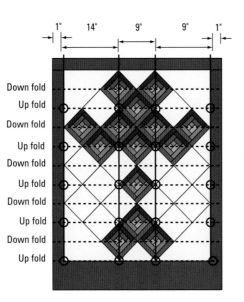

Lift lines placed at centers of block.

Mark the lift line positions and the positions of the rings (they go on each up fold). I generally use a red pen to note the battens (on the up folds and down folds) and lift rings. This is your blueprint for making your shade. Make a drawing that includes the window with the shade fully raised and mark where the shade will be mounted. This shows how much glass will be bare when your Window Hanging is fully raised.

If You Use Full-Block Folds with an Odd Number of Rows

When the shade is folded on the full-block, both the up folds and the down folds are at the bottom of the block. That is, the bottom of a row of blocks might be on an up fold or a down fold. Since you need an equal number of up folds and down folds, you have to be concerned with the number of rows.

When you have an even number of rows of blocks, the lowest row of rings is placed at the bottom of the lowest row of blocks. This creates the first up fold. The bottom of the next row of blocks is a down fold. When fully raised, the entire top row of blocks shows.

When you have an odd number of rows of blocks and are folding on the full-block, you have to modify the placement of the lift rings. If the lowest row of lift rings is placed at the bottom of the lowest row of blocks, you will not have an equal number of up and down folds. You must therefore place the lowest row of lift rings at the bottom of the **second** row of blocks. When fully raised, the entire top row of blocks shows as with an even number of rows.

If you look closely at the illustration, you will see that you have two layout choices for every block size (block height) when you are folding the Window Hanging on the full block.

1. You can have an even number of rows with a large bottom border

2. You can have an odd number of rows with a small bottom border. (Must be at least 1").

Since the bottom border for an even number of rows must be greater than the block height, you can **always** place another row of blocks on top of the bottom border, making a Window Hanging with an odd number of rows. Both versions of the layout will look the same when fully raised.

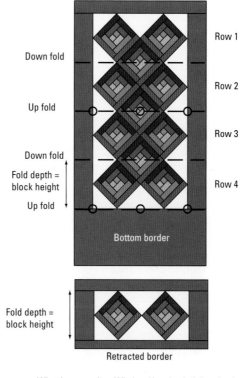

What is seen when Window Hanging is fully raised = top border + block height + retracted border

1. Full block fold: EVEN number of rows.

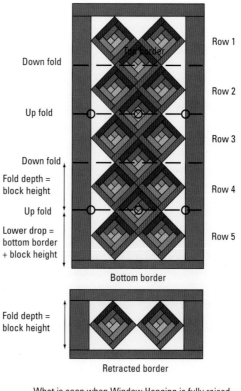

What is seen when Window Hanging is fully raised = top border + block height + bottom border

2. Full block fold: ODD number of rows with a small bottom border.

1. **Even number of rows with large bottom border.**

Odd number of rows with one row of blocks placed over large bottom border.

2. **Odd number of rows with small bottom border.**

SUMMARY

Draw the shade to scale.

Verify First Vertical Layout Rule: top border must be longer than the mounting board length + lift ring diameter (or greater than 4")

Verify Second Layout Rule:
Half-block fold:
bottom border must be longer than $1/2$ block height + 1"

Full-block fold - even number of rows:
bottom border must be longer than block height + 1"

Full-block fold - odd number of rows:
bottom border must be longer than 1"

Check the finished length = top border + (block height x number of rows) + bottom border

Check the finished width = side border + (block width x number of columns) + side border

Draw the fully raised shade.

Figuring Fabric YARDAGE and Hardware

In this chapter, we will complete the Fabric and Hardware Shopping Lists, which summarize your yardage and hardware needs. Make a copy of the forms, which are in the Appendix on page 106 and 107.

Determining Your Block Fabric Yardages

Each of the projects includes yardage tables. Refer to these for your shade. If you make a Window Hanging with a different block, calculate your own yardage by drawing your block, adding seam allowances and figuring requirements for the total number of blocks.

Determining Your Border Yardages

Your final drawing of your Window Hanging is your best guide to figuring border yardage. Work with each fabric separately. Unless you know the actual useable width of a fabric, use a fabric width of 40", rather than the 45" noted on the bolt.

Your borders will be attached to the inner front using a squared (or butted) seam. You will be attaching the side borders first, then the bottom border, and finally the top border. I like to use an accent border between the inner front and the border. An accent border width of $1/2$ " to 1" sets off the design. When you make your Window Hanging, you will adjust the border sizes after you have sewn the inner front (blocks, sashings, setting triangles, etc.) together to compensate for any inaccuracies in your block sizes. Our calculations will include sufficient extra inches to make sure you do not get caught short of fabric.

> When describing borders, length refers to the long dimension, and width refers to the shorter dimension regardless of the direction they are running. So when calculating the top and bottom borders, you use the finished width of the Window Hanging to calculate the cut length of the borders. Similary, use the length of the borders to calculate the cut width.

Determining Border Widths and Lengths

Cut one (1) top border
Calculate the *cut width* of the top border by adding together:

◆ The *length* of the top border as calculated in your layout form

◆ $1/4$" seam allowance

◆ 3" for loop fastener attachment

Calculate the *cut length* of the top border by adding together:

◆ The *finished width* of the Window Hanging

◆ 2" to turn around to the back (1" on each side)

◆ 3" extra to allow for squaring the front

Cut one (1) bottom border
Calculate the *cut width* of the bottom border by adding together:

◆ The *length* of the bottom border as calculated in your layout form

◆ $1/4$" seam allowance

◆ 6" for hem (double 3")

If you are using an accent border, you need to subtract the *finished width* of the accent border from the bottom border *cut width*.

Calculate the *cut length* of the bottom border by adding together:

◆ The *finished width* of the Window Hanging

◆ 2" to turn around to the back (1" on each side)

◆ 3" extra to allow for squaring the front

TIP

If you are making more than one shade, be sure and calculate the total amount of fabric and hardware required for all of the shades, not just for one.

Cut two (2) side borders

Calculate the *cut width* of the side borders by adding together:

◆ The *width* of the side border as calculated in your layout form

◆ $1/4$" seam allowance

◆ 1" to turn around to the back

◆ 2" extra to allow for block irregularities

Calculate the *cut length* of the side borders by adding 6" to the inner front length of your Window Hanging.

Cut four (4) accent borders

Calculate the *cut width* of the accent border by adding $1/2$" to its finished width for seam allowances.

Calculate the *cut length* for sides by adding 3" to the inner front length (cut two).

Calculate the *cut length* for top and bottom by adding 4" to the inner front width (cut two).

Cut length of top border = finished width + 5″

Cut width of top border = length from layout form + 3 $1/4$″

 KEY : Calculated size of border

Additional fabric needed for seam allowances, hems, turn backs, etc.

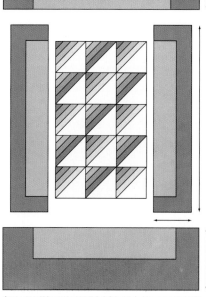

Cut length of side border = inner front length + 6″

Cut width of side border = width from layout form + 3 $1/4$″

Cut width of bottom border = length from layout form + 6$1/4$″ - finished size of accent border

Cut length of bottom border = finished width + 5″

Calculating Window Hanging borders.

Laying Out and Cutting the Border Fabric

You will be using large pieces of fabric for the borders and possibly for background pieces. You should always place the longest dimension on-grain. Your Window Hanging will hang correctly if you always follow this rule. If possible, also cut your narrow accent border on-grain as well. If you decide to piece the accent border, make bias seams, which are less noticeable.

Draw out the borders on paper to determine the required yardage. Mark dimensions clearly and keep this drawing. You will need it when you make your shade. Calculate your yardages and put them on the Fabric Shopping list. (Appendix page 107)

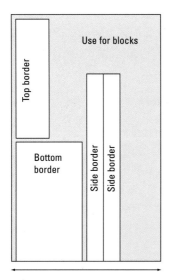

Assume 40" usable width of fabric for laying out borders.

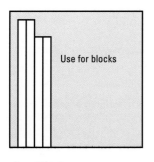

Accent borders

Lay out borders on the lengthwise grain.

Background pieces

If you are designing your own project and it has background pieces, decide how you will piece them. Write down the finished dimensions of each piece.

If you are using setting triangles and corner triangles with an on-point design, I suggest that you float the design by cutting oversized triangles. See page 73 for directions. Fill in the background piece fabric requirements in the Fabric Shopping list.

Lining Requirements

Choosing lining

Choose the lining fabric carefully. It **must** be designed to block ultraviolet light, or your front fabrics will fade. I highly recommend that you use Roc-lon® Thermalsuede® lining from Rockland Industries, Inc. It is available in white and ivory in 48" and 54" widths. Most fabric stores that sell home decorating fabrics carry it. Thermalsuede is a 50% cotton/50% polyester, closely woven fabric with a soft plastic backing that adds stability to the cloth and prevents sun-fading of the front fabrics. It also acts as an excellent insulation against heat and cold. One other property that I find particularly attractive is that it is light-filtering, so that you get a reasonable amount of light through the shade when it is lowered. This gives a special effect to your Window Hanging, making it appear like a stained glass window. You cannot see through the shades, so they provide privacy when down.

If you decide to use drapery lining that is not coated, cut the lining so that the lengthwise grain of the fabric runs vertically in your shade. Use one piece of fabric whenever possible since you will be able to see any seams when the shade is backlit.

Cutting the lining and working with Thermalsuede

Thermalsuede lining, shrinks up to 3%, so cutting instructions include extra inches to allow for this. I never pre-wash the lining, but do steam iron it thoroughly, which shrinks it. You will often be sewing with the plastic side of the lining facing up, which tends to grab at the presser foot. Use a Teflon foot or a walking foot if possible. If you do

TIP

It helps to use oversized background pieces so that you can square up the inner front of your Window Hanging. Add at least 1" to each dimension to allow for this.

TIP

If you must piece the lining, try to place the seams directly behind either the side or bottom border seams.

TIP

If you are making
more than one
shade – multiply
your fabric
and hardware
requirements.

not have either of these presser feet, place some adding machine paper on top of the lining and sew right through it. Remove the paper by tearing along the stitched seam.

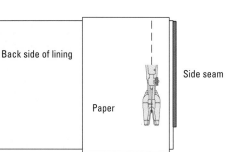

Back side of lining

Paper

Side seam

**Use adding machine paper when sewing
Thermalsuede to prevent pulling.**

Determining lining width and length

Calculate the *cut lining length* by adding together:

◆ The finished length of the Window Hanging

◆ 6" (double 3" hem)

◆ 2" top fold over

◆ 4" extra to allow for shrinkage

Calculate the *cut lining width* by adding together:

◆ The finished width of the Window Hanging

◆ 3" extra to allow for shrinkage

Sketch your lining cutting diagram and calculate your yardage. Enter this value into the Fabric Shopping list.

Hardware and Supply Requirements

Complete the rest of the Hardware Shopping List using the following guidelines. See the Resources section on page 110 for suppliers. You will be referring to your final design drawing for your own specific information.

Hook and loop fastener

Length of hook and loop fastener: Add 2" to the finished width of Window Hanging.

Battens

Length of each batten: Add 1" to the finished width of Window Hanging.

Number of battens: You will need one batten for each fold.

Lift rings

You need lift rings on all of the up folds for each lift line

Number of lift rings: You can count the number of rings on your final drawing or calculate by multiplying the number of up folds by the number of lift lines.

Pulleys

Number of pulleys: You need one pulley for each lift line.

Lift cord

Each lift cord runs the length of the Window Hanging, across the top, and back down the length on the other side.

To calculate the amount of lift cord needed:

Multiply the finished length of the Window Hanging by 2, then add the finished width of the Hanging. Multiply this number by the number of lift lines. This will allow extra cord that can be trimmed after the Window Hanging is mounted.

Weight rod

Length of weight rod: Add 1" to the finished width of the Window Hanging.

Mounting board

Length of mounting board: Add 1" to the finished width of the Window Hanging.

Fabric to cover mounting board

You can use remnants from your shade fabric, or use lightweight white cloth. Measure the size of your mounting board. Then calculate:

Length of cover fabric: Add 5" to the length of mounting board

Width of cover fabric: Add $3/4$" to the circumference of the mounting board

Cord drop and cleat

You will need one of each for each shade.

Making a WINDOW HANGING

Allow for Squaring

As you read through the projects, you probably will have noticed that you will continually be trimming your blocks and assembled pieces into perfect rectangles. Because fabric is soft and stretches and shrinks as you sew the many pieces into the finished front, you will make your life easier if you oversize the large background pieces. I add at least an inch in each dimension to large rectangular pieces. One of my favorite "looks" for a Window Hanging is to place the block on point and then fill in the outside of the pattern with oversized setting triangles. This is known as "floating the blocks."

Make setting triangles by cutting squares diagonally twice.

Size to cut square =

◆ multiply the **finished** block size by 1.41
◆ round up to the nearest 1/8" (see chart for 1/8" decimals)
◆ add 1.75", this will add the 1/4" seams and make the triangle oversized.

Make corner triangles by cutting squares diagonally once.

Size to cut square =

◆ multiply the **finished** block size by .71
◆ round up to the nearest 1/8" (see chart for 1/8" decimals)
◆ add 1.375", this will add the 1/4" seams and make the triangle oversized.

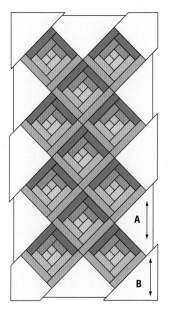

Floating the blocks.

1/8"	.125"
1/4"	.25"
3/8"	.375"
1/2"	.5
5/8"	.625
3/4"	.75"
7/8"	.875"

Fraction to decimal conversion.

Allowances for side seams, top turnover and hem

The front of the Window Hanging will be trimmed to the finished dimensions plus allowances as shown below. The lining is trimmed to 1" narrower than the front width.

Finished width from window measurement

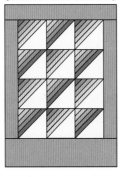

Finished length from window measurement

Finished front.

Amounts added to finished sizes to allow for hem and turn-arounds. Also referred to as trimmed length or width

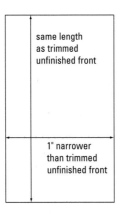

³/4" turnaround

1" turnaround   1" turnaround

6" (double 3" hem)

Trimmed unfinished front.

same length as trimmed unfinished front

1" narrower than trimmed unfinished front

Trimmed lining.

Making hems

A double 3" bottom hem is used for both the front and the lining. To make the hem, turn up the lower raw edge 6", wrong sides together, and press. Open up the first fold and turn the raw edge in to meet the pressed fold and press again. Refold and machine stitch close to the second fold.

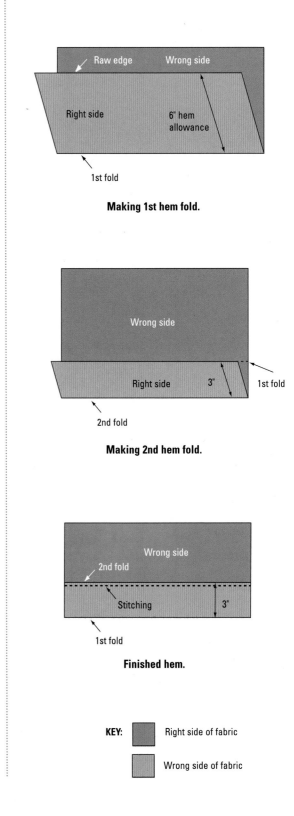

Raw edge   Wrong side

Right side   6" hem allowance

1st fold

Making 1st hem fold.

Wrong side

Right side   3"   1st fold

2nd fold

Making 2nd hem fold.

Wrong side

2nd fold

Stitching   3"

1st fold

Finished hem.

KEY: Right side of fabric

Wrong side of fabric

Step 1. Make and Square the Blocks

You make the front of a Window Hanging much the same as you make the top of a quilt. You then sew that front into a Roman shade. Refer to the sketch of your final Window Hanging and your fabric layouts.

Count the number of required blocks. Cut out the fabric pieces and assemble using a $1/4$" seam. Stack all of the blocks up and choose the smallest one. Square if necessary and then measure the dimensions. Trim the remaining blocks to the same size.

It is more important to have all of the blocks square and the same size than to have all of the points in the design at the correct locations.

The block size may be slightly off from your desired dimensions. For example, your "9 inch" blocks may be 8 $3/4$". That is okay. Having several 9" blocks, several 8 $7/8$" blocks and several 8 $3/4$" blocks is not okay.

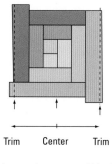

Trim   Center   Trim

Measure from center of block

Square and trim all of the blocks symmetrically to the size of the smallest block.

Step 2. Assemble and Square the Inner Front

Using your design layout, assemble the blocks. Cut and use any required background pieces to complete your design. Place the inner front on a large working surface. Carefully smooth out flat. Using a carpenter's square and one or more long rulers, square up the inner front. Use a disappearing marker to mark the trim lines. You want all width measurements to be at least within $1/4$" of each other. The same is true for the length measurements. If they are not, your marked inner front is not square. Re-mark and re-measure. When you are happy with your measurements, trim the inner front width as marked.

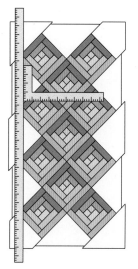

2a. Using a carpenter's square and long ruler, mark one edge with a disappearing marker.

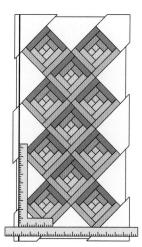

2b. Mark the other edges, making sure they are square.

Try not to "ease and stretch" your blocks to make the seams and points meet. This distorts the fabric. You want your front to be flat when you lay it on a table. It is better to have your points and seams mismatched than to have "mountains" sticking out from your shade.

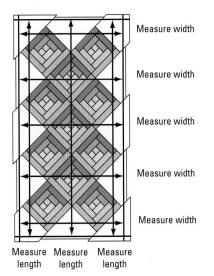

Measure width

Measure width

Measure width

Measure width

Measure width

Measure length   Measure length   Measure length

2c. Measure both the width and length in at least three places.

TIP

Do not trim the extensions on the top and bottom border pieces.

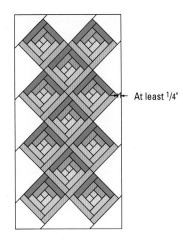

At least 1/4"

2d. Trim the inner front along your marker. Try to leave at least $1/4$" all the way around your blocks.

If some parts of the blocks are sewn on the bias, one side of the inner front often will be larger than the opposite side. You must trim this down at this stage. You may lose points because they may end up closer to the trimmed edge than $1/4$". The bottom row of blocks may appear to be narrower than the top. If you have used oversized background pieces, you can float the design by making the trimmed edge more than $1/4$". This looks nice and makes squaring the inner front much easier. The inner front width **must** be square before you add the borders.

If you compare your actual inner front measurements, they will almost certainly be different from your ideal values that you have in your final drawing of your Window Hanging. Usually the actual measurements are smaller. Your block often shrinks because it is difficult to fully flatten the seams when pressing and squaring the inner front. This results in a loss of width and length.

What does it mean for our inner front dimensions to differ from our calculated value? Since the finished dimensions of our Window Hanging are fixed, the border widths will change. Usually they will get larger, which is why we added several inches to our border dimensions when we calculated yardage. If you thought you would skimp and buy only the "correct" yardage, you will probably be caught short at this stage.

Step 3. Attach the Borders

If you are using an accent border cut the strips then attach, using a $1/4$" seam. Cut your strips according to your fabric layout drawing.

Cut your border pieces according to your fabric layout drawing. Mark and sew a double 3" hem (see Illustration on page 74) in the bottom border before attaching.

Trim   Trim

Trim   Trim

3a. Attach side accent border. Trim ends.

3b. Attach top and bottom accent border. Trim ends.

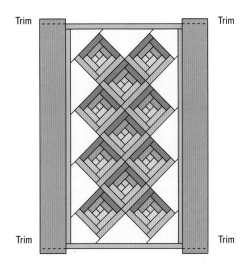

3c. Attach side borders. Trim ends.

3d. Hem bottom border. Attach top and bottom borders. DO NOT trim.

Step 4. Measure and Square the Completed Front

Place the front on a large working surface. Carefully smooth flat. You will be trimming the **sides** to the front trimmed width. The top will be trimmed **after** attaching the lining.

Front trimmed width = finished width + 2"

Use the center of the **inner front width** to begin your measurements. Mark both sides of the shade. Now stand back and look at the front.

Are the side borders approximately the same width?

Does everything look symmetrical?

Is the trim width equal to your finished width plus 2"?

Carefully trim your side borders.

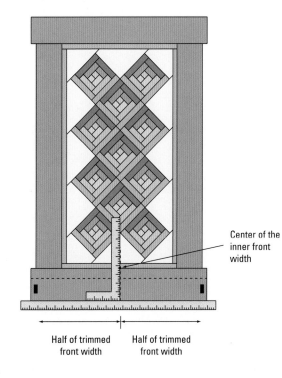

4a. Trimmed width = finished width + 2".
Mark the center of the inner front with a straight pin, then mark where to trim the sides.

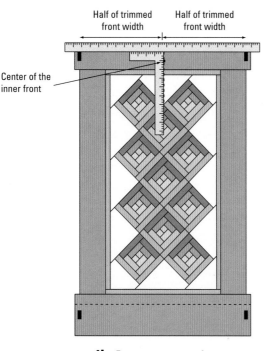

Half of trimmed
front width

Half of trimmed
front width

Center of the
inner front

4b. Repeat process at the top.

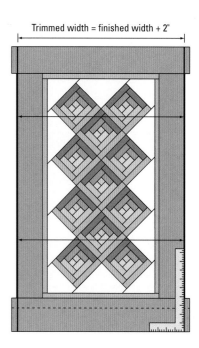

Trimmed width = finished width + 2"

4d. Check that front is square and that all widths
measure within 1/4" before trimming.

4c. Mark the entire trim lines.

Step 5. Line the Window Hanging

Cut and hem the lining

Refer to page 71 for tips on working with
Thermalsuede. Carefully trim away the selvages
parallel to the edge. Using a carpenter's square,
square up one end. Cut out the lining according to
your lining cutting diagram. Thoroughly press the
lining using a medium setting on your iron. Spray
the lining with water and press every square inch
to shrink it. If necessary, join two pieces using a
1/4" seam and press to one side. Sew a double 3"
hem in the bottom using white thread. Press thoroughly. Now trim the sides of the hemmed lining:

Trimmed lining width = trimmed front width - 1"

Use a carpenter's square to make sure that your
lining is square. Use the trimmed width measurement of your actual front, raw-edge to raw-edge,
and make the lining one inch narrower.

Join lining and front at sides

Lay the pieced front right side up on a work surface, with the bottom (hem) to your left. Lay the
lining right side down on top of the pieced front.
The bottom hems will both be to your left. The

bottom of the lining should be $1/2$" above the bottom of the front. Pin every 2" to 3" along the entire edge of the lining. Also pin the front and the lining together in several places towards the center to stabilize and prevent pulling during stitching. Using a $3/4$" **seam**, sew the first side seam beginning at the hem edge and ending at the top edge. Press the seam flat towards the lining.

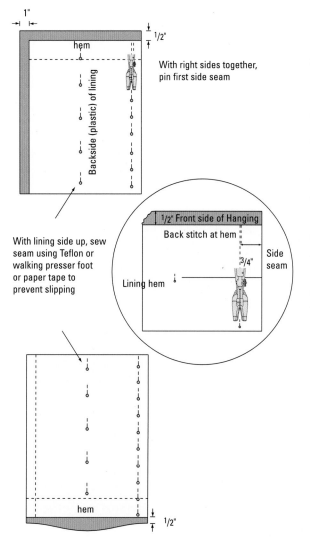

With lining side up, sew seam using Teflon or walking presser foot or paper tape to prevent slipping

With right sides together, pin and sew second side seam.

With right sides together and with the lining still on top, pin the second side seam. Once again, make sure the bottom of the lining is $1/2$" above the bottom of the pieced front. This time you will be sewing from the top of the shade to the hem. Backstitch at the hem. Using an ironing board, press the second seam flat towards the lining.

Turn the Window Hanging right side out. Place it upside down (lining facing up) on a large work surface. Smooth into a rectangle. You should have a $1/4$" overlap of the front fabric around to the back on each side. Pull the Window Hanging firmly from both sides to achieve this. Make sure that the bottom of the lining is $1/2$" above the front. Press thoroughly. Pin in several places before turning over. Press again, being careful not to iron directly on the pins. Carefully smooth the Window Hanging and measure the width in at least three places. Verify that the measurements are within $1/4$" of your finished width. If they are not, remove stitching, and re-sew the side seams.

Close the top with loop fastener

With the front side up, smooth into place. Turn up the hem and make sure that the lining and front fabric are $1/2$" apart along the entire width of the Window Hanging. It is important that the center not sag and that the lining not fall below the front fabric. Carefully smooth the Window Hanging up towards the top edge. Pin the front fabric and lining together about 4" below the top edges at frequent intervals. Mark and trim the top of the Window Hanging.

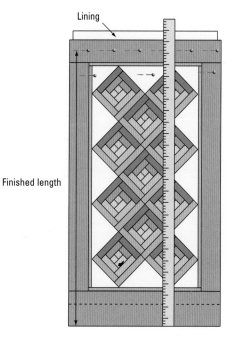

5a. Mark finished length with straight pins.

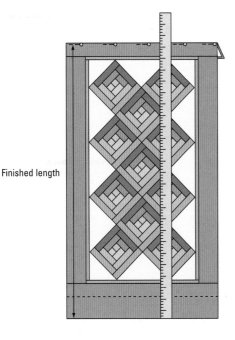

5b. Press under top turnover and remeasure finished length.

Finished length

5d. Sew top of loop fastener, measure finished width and then sew bottom of loop fastener.

pin
every 2"

loop
fastener

1/4"

1/2"

3/4"

Finished length

5c. Trim top turn to 3/4", fold under and pin loop fastener on top of fold in the back side of the shade.

Cut the loop fastener 1" longer than the finished width. Using thread that matches the front fabric, sew the top of the loop fastener to the Window Hanging, backstitching at each end. Go slowly, holding the fabrics both behind and in front of the machine needle and tugging gently to avoid slippage. Since you are sewing three dissimilar materials together it is easy to end up with a much narrower finished width at the top of your Window Hanging. Do not trim the excess loop fastener. Remove all of the pins and measure the finished width. If it is still correct, sew the bottom edge of the loop fastener, backstitching at each end. Measure the finished width. If the measurement is not correct, remove the stitching and re-sew. Trim the excess loop fastener. While the colored thread is still in your sewing machine, fold the bottom of the side seams up and tack.

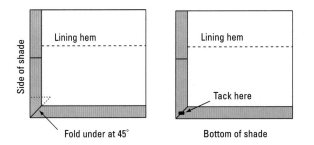

Fold under at 45°   Bottom of shade

One last time, measure your Window Hanging. Smooth it out on a large table. Measure the width and length in at least three places. Verify that these correspond to your desired finished dimensions.

Step 6. Attach Battens and Rings

Make all of your measurements for your hardware now. You can make the mounting board while the batten glue is drying. Use the Hardware Worksheet that is contained in the Appendix, page 106. If you are making more than one Window Hanging, you must do this separately for each shade. Also mark the center of the finished width at the top of the Window Hanging on the loop fastener using a pencil. You will use this mark when you attach the Window Hanging onto the mounting board.

Using wire cutters, cut the wooden or plastic battens to $1/2$" less than the finished width of the Window Hanging. For shades wider than 60", splice the plastic battens using metal splints. Tape the seam with a small piece of cellophane tape.

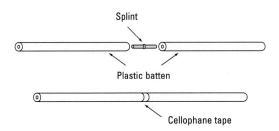

Turn the Window Hanging **inside out** and lay it on your worktable with the back side of the pieced fabric facing up. Smooth the edges so that the sides lie as flat as possible and the border fabrics are even on each side. You will be using the borders and the design to center the battens. Referring to your final design for locations, attach

the battens in place using glue designed for attaching sequins to fabric. Place a very small dot of glue (the size of a small pea) on a seam, being careful not to have the glue run over to the front fabric. Glue every 6" to 12" if possible. Let the battens dry thoroughly for a minimum of four hours, preferable overnight.

Inside of Window Hanging

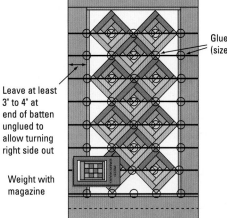

Glue locations (size is exaggerated)

Leave at least 3" to 4" at end of batten unglued to allow turning right side out

Weight with magazine

Glue the battens on the inside of the Window Hanging.

After the glue has completely dried, carefully turn the Window Hanging right side out by reaching up inside the shade, holding onto the loop fastener top, and gently pulling the Window Hanging right side out. The battens will bend slightly to allow this. The battens must be on the front side of the side seams. Check each one through the fabric and adjust if necessary. If you misjudged the centering of a batten, carefully trim off the end using wire cutters. Be very careful not to cut the fabric while you are doing this. Smooth the Window Hanging carefully on the worktable and pin in several locations in preparation for sewing on the rings.

Referring to your final design drawing, sew the lift rings in place, using thread that matches the front fabric in each location. The rings will be sewn on every other batten along the lift lines. The thread should loop around the internal battens. The stitches will show on the front of the shade, but you should be able to make the visible portion less than $1/4$". (See page 82)

Spray the front of your Window Hanging with Scotchgard™ or Quiltgard™. Let it dry completely.

TIP

Using a weight, such as a book, will help keep the battens in contact with the fabric and the glue.

TIP

You may have to mark the center of the blocks for a half-fold design. Use a long ruler and make a small pencil mark on the seams where you will glue the battens.

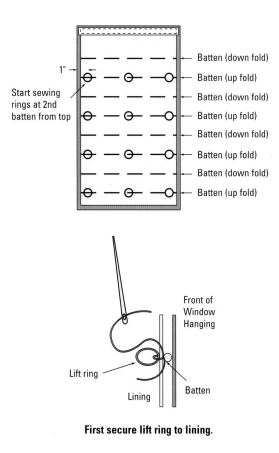

1"
Start sewing
rings at 2nd
batten from top

Batten (down fold)
Batten (up fold)
Batten (down fold)
Batten (up fold)
Batten (down fold)
Batten (up fold)
Batten (down fold)
Batten (up fold)

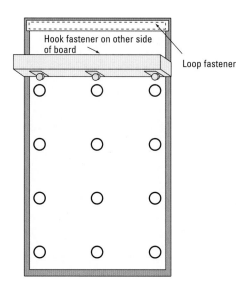

Hook fastener on other side
of board

Loop fastener

**Lay mounting board just above lift rings
to mark position of pulleys.**

Front of
Window
Hanging

Lift ring

Lining

Batten

First secure lift ring to lining.

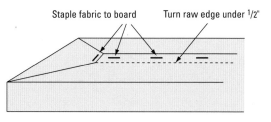

Staple fabric to board   Turn raw edge under 1/2"

Covering the mounting board with fabric.

Front of
Window
Hanging

Lift ring

Lining

Batten

**Sew lift ring to Hanging, passing thread through
to front and back around batten to lining.**

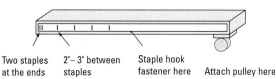

Two staples
at the ends

2"– 3" between
staples

Staple hook
fastener here

Attach pulley here

Projected mounting board.

Step 7. Make the Mounting Board

Using a saw, cut the mounting board to ¼" less
than the width of the Window Hanging at the top.
Cut the covering fabric to the size given on the
Hardware Worksheet. Fold and staple the fabric
onto the mounting board. Staple the hook fastener
to the front of the mounting board. Mark the center of the board on the hook fastener with a pencil.
You will use this mark when you attach the
Window Hanging to the mounting board.

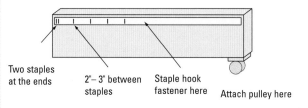

Two staples
at the ends

2"– 3" between
staples

Staple hook
fastener here

Attach pulley here

Flat mounting board.

Lay the Window Hanging face down on your worktable. Lay the mounting board across a row of rings. Carefully mark the position of the pulleys. Attach the pulleys to the bottom of the mounting board using small screws. If you will be using an outside or hybrid mount for your shade, make side flaps out of the border fabric to cover the hardware.

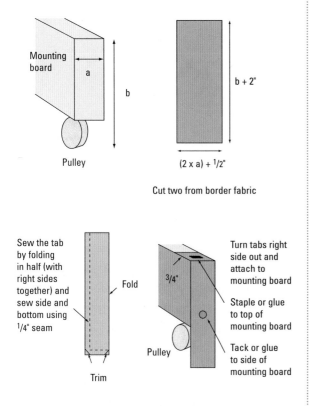

Cut two from border fabric

Make side tabs to cover the hardware for an outside or hybrid mount mounting board.

Look at the front of the Window Hanging and use a safety pin to mark the side on which the pull cord will be. String the shade by laying the Window Hanging face down on your worktable. Place the mounting board onto the top of the shade, mating the hook and loop fasteners. Tie cord with a square knot to the lowest ring in each column. Then thread it through all the rings in a column and the pulleys. Extend each cord about 10" past the desired finished length of the cord.

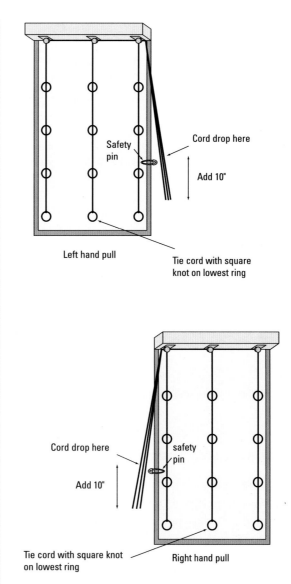

String the lift cords.

Test your shade by pulling on the lift cords with one hand while holding the mounting board with the other hand. If your shade is large, you may want to have someone help you with this. Check that the shade lifts evenly and that the cords go through every ring. Now go to your window and hold the Window Hanging up. Make sure that it is the correct size.

Remove the shade from the mounting board, carefully removing the lift cords from the pulleys, making sure they stay threaded through the lift rings. Loosely tie all of the cords into a knot at the top of the shade so that they don't slip out of the rings.

Using a hacksaw, cut the weight rod to the length determined by the Hardware Worksheet. File off any burrs. Slip the rod into the lining hem pocket.

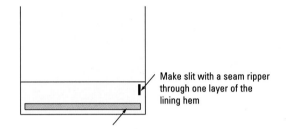

Make slit with a seam ripper through one layer of the lining hem

Weight rod will drop to bottom of lining hem pocket.

Step 8. Install Your Window Hanging

Attach the mounting board at the window using screws that go directly through the mounting board into the wall or window trim. If desired, you can use angle irons. Use a level to make sure that the mounting board is installed on the horizontal.

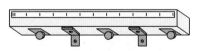

Mounting board screwed directly into wall or trim.

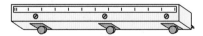

Mounting board using angle irons.

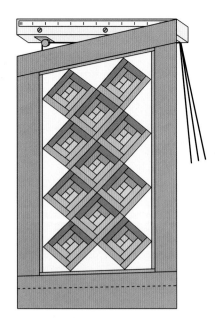

Loosely attach the Window Hanging at the side where the pull cord will be.

Thread the lift cords through the pulleys by loosely attaching the side of the shade where the pull cord will be to the mounting board. Fold down the other side of the shade, untie the loose knot, and thread the lift cords on that side of the Window Hanging through the pulleys. Attach that side of the top of the shade and pull down the other half of the shade to continue threading the cords through the pulleys. Test the shade by pulling on all cords. Loosely tie all of the lift cords into a knot near the top of the shade. Correctly position the shade onto the mounting board by matching the center of the Window Hanging (which you marked with a pencil) with the center of the mounting board. Carefully mate the fasteners, gently stretching the shade as you move towards the edges. Make sure that the mounting board is fully covered and that the top of the shade is even. Untie the loose knot, gently pull all cords taut and carefully tie a knot near the top of the shade. Lift and lower the shade to make sure that it is retracting evenly.

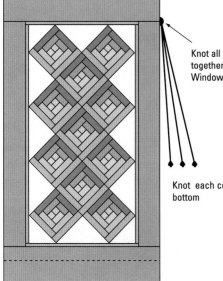

Knot all lift cords together at top of Window Hanging

Knot each cord at bottom

Cord pull method 1.

Finish off the cord pull using one of the methods shown.

Wrap the cords around a cleat when the shade is up. When the shade is raised, there will be a loop above the knot to the top of the shade. When the shade is lowered there is no loop.

Small children have on occasion inserted their heads through these loops and strangled them selves. If you have small children, place the cleat as high as possible on the wall and loop the loose cord up over the cleat. Or you can tuck the cord into a fold in the shade to keep it out of the way.

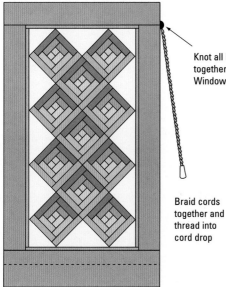

Knot all lift cords together at top of Window Hanging

Braid cords together and thread into cord drop

Cord pull method 2

Finish off the lift cords.

Making a VALANCE

The following are general instructions for making a valance. Instructions for making a valance using the Illusions block can be found starting on page 54.

Step 1. Decide How to Mount Your Valance

You have two options for mounting your valance: inside and outside. On a bare window, you can use either an inside or outside mount. However, if there are existing window treatments, you will usually use an outside, projection mount. If you need a board that projects further than a 1x2, you can use a standard 1x3 (which usually measures 3/4" by 2 1/4"). Another standard board size that you can use is 1x6 (usually 3/4" by 5 1/2"). If you want another projection depth, a full-service lumber store will "rip" a 1x6 down to a smaller size for a nominal fee.

Measure your Window

Measure the top of the window and the existing treatments in three dimensions (width, length, and depth). Decide on the finished width and the finished length of the front of your valance. Normally the length of a valance will be between 12" and 24".

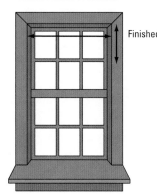

Inside mount.

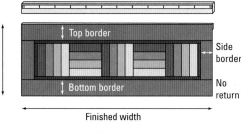

Inside mount.

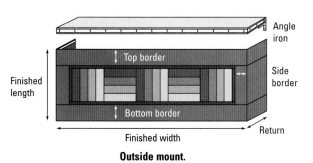

Outside mount.

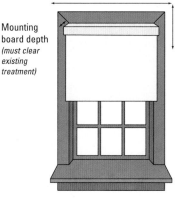

Ouside mount over existing window treatment.

Step 2. Design the Valance Front

Design the front of the valance by using the Horizontal Layout Form in the Appendix on page 104. Vary the block size until you get a pleasing design. Determine the top and bottom borders. You will usually have only a single row of blocks. Draw your valance, noting block size, border widths, finished width, finished length and returns. If you have not used the Horizontal Layout Form to make a Window Hanging, refer to page 64 for information on using the Horizontal Layout Form.

Step 3. Calculate Fabric and Hardware Requirements

Determine the block fabric yardages by adding quarter-inch seams to your block diagram. Use the drawing of your valance to figure the border yardage.

If you are using an outside mount, the size of the return will be added to the side border measurement when you are calculating how to cut the valance borders. As with the Window Hangings, the cutting instructions for borders includes allowances that compensate for block size irregularities and give you room to square your valance front before you join it to the lining.

Cutting Instructions for Borders

Cut two (2) side borders
Calculate the *cut width* of the side borders by adding together:

◆ The *width* of the side border as calculated in your layout form

◆ The size of the return

◆ 3 1/4" (1" turn around, 2" extra to allow for irregularities, and 1/4" seam allowance.)

Calculate the *cut length* of the side borders by adding 3" to the inner front length.

Cut one (1) top border
Calculate the *cut width* of the top border by adding together:

◆ The *length* of the top border as calculated in your layout form

◆ 3 1/4" (3" for the hook and loop fastener and 1/4" seam allowance)

Calculate the *cut length* of the top border by adding together:

◆ The *finished width* of the valance

◆ The size of both returns

◆ 5" (1" turn around on each side and 3" to allow for irregularities)

TIP

Pay close attention to the **cut** width and **cut** length dimensions for your side borders. A valance with a large return will usually have side borders with a cut width that is larger than the cut length.

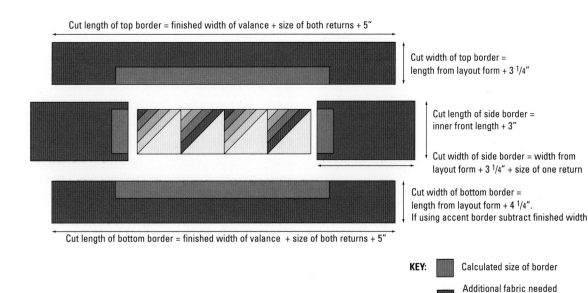

Cut length of top border = finished width of valance + size of both returns + 5"

Cut width of top border = length from layout form + 3 1/4"

Cut length of side border = inner front length + 3"

Cut width of side border = width from layout form + 3 1/4" + size of one return

Cut width of bottom border = length from layout form + 4 1/4". If using accent border subtract finished width

Cut length of bottom border = finished width of valance + size of both returns + 5"

KEY: Calculated size of border

Additional fabric needed for seam allowances, hems, turn backs, returns, etc.

Cut one (1) bottom border

Calculate the *cut width* of the bottom border by adding together

◆ The *length* of the bottom border as calculated in your layout form

◆ 4 $1/4$" (4" for double 2" hem and $1/4$" seam allowance)

> If you are using an accent border, subtract its finished width from the width of the bottom border.

Calculate the *cut length* of the bottom border by adding together:

◆ The finished width of the valance

◆ The size of both returns

◆ 5" (1" turn around on each side and 3" to allow for irregularities)

Cut four (4) accent borders

Calculate the *cut width* of the accent border by adding $1/2$" to its finished width for seam allowances.

Calculate the *cut length* for sides by adding 3" to the inner front length (cut two).

Calculate the *cut length* for top and bottom by adding 4" to the inner front width (cut two).

Draw out the borders on paper to determine the required yardages. Label the dimensions clearly and use this drawing when you make your valance.

TIP

You should make the mounting board before completing the valance so that you have the actual measurements around the three sides of the board when you trim your borders.

Cutting Instructions for Lining

Calculate the *cut width* of the lining by adding together:

◆ The *finished width* of the valance

◆ The size of both returns

◆ 4" for shrinkage

Calculate the *cut length* of the lining by adding 7" to the *finished length* of the valance

Hardware Requirements

You will need the following items to make your valance:

Hook and loop fastener
Length of hook and loop fastener: Add 2" to the finished width of the valance plus both returns.

Mounting Board
Length of mounting board: Subtract a quarter inch from the finished width of the valance

Width of mounting board: This is determined by the type of mounting and the existing window treatments.

Fabric to cover board
Calculate the *length* of cover fabric by adding 5" to the length of mounting board

Calculate the *width* of cover fabric by adding $3/4$" to the circumference of the board

Step 4. Construct the Mounting Board

If your board is not already cut to the correct length (a quarter inch less than the finished width of the valance), cut the board using a hand saw. Cover the board with fabric by following the instructions on page 82. Staple the hook fastener to the returns and front of the mounting board.

Step 5. Sew the Valance Front

Make and square all the blocks as described on page 75. Sew the blocks together to make the inner front. It is important that the blocks and the resulting inner front be square.

Step 6. Add the Borders

Use your border fabric drawings to cut out your border pieces. Sew the side accent borders to the inner front, then attach the top and bottom accent borders.

Sew the side borders to the valance inner front. Hem the bottom border with a double 2" hem before sewing it to the valance front (see page 74 for details on making a down fold hem). Sew the top border to the valance front. Do not trim the side seams!

Step 7. Trim the Valance

Using a cloth tape measure, measure the sides and front of the mounting board (which you have already covered using the directions described on pages 82-83) directly on top of the hook fastener.

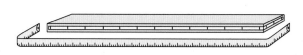

Measure the actual complete finished length of the mounting board, including returns, before trimming sides of valance.

Use the same cloth tape measure to mark the side trim line of the valance front, adding 2" (a 1" turn-around for each side seam) to the measured length of the mounting board (including returns). Trim the sides of the front as marked.

Step 8. Cut and Sew the Lining

Read the section on working with lining fabric starting on page 71 before cutting your lining fabric.

Hem the lining with a double 2" hem (see page 74 for details on making a double fold hem), and trim the width to 1" narrower than the trimmed pieced front.

Sew the side seams and close the top using the loop fastener. Refer to page 77 and 80 for instructions on sewing the side seams and attaching the loop fastener.

Step 9. Finish the Valance

Thoroughly press your completed valance. Mark the center of the valance using a pencil on the loop fastener. Mark the center of the board on the hook fastener. Spray the front of your valance with a stain-resistant spray and let it dry completely.

Install the mounting board at the window. Correctly position the shade onto the mounting board by lining the center of the valance with the center of the mounting board. Carefully mate the fasteners, gently stretching the valance as you move towards the edges. Make sure that the mounting board is fully covered and that the top of the valance is even.

Other IDEAS: Challenges and Opportunities

In the preceeding projects, we covered several block configurations: square straight-set (Shadows), square on-point (Oriental Delight), and rectangular (Illusions). As you continue designing new Window Hangings, you will quickly discover that there are many other types of designs that will work. You can use any pattern, as long as you can identify a vertical repeat.

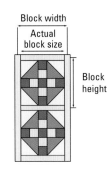

Add half the width of the sashing to block height and width.

Sashing

You may want to include a sashing in your inner front. A sashing is the fabric used to frame and separate the blocks. The easiest way to lay out your Window Hanging is to add half of the width of the sashing on all sides of the block to the block size. This works for both a straight set and an on-point design.

For a straight-set design, your fold lines will go through the center of the sashing strips. Plan the order in which you sew the strips onto your blocks so that you have seams where you can glue your battens. In the illustration, the Churn Dash blocks are fully pieced, and then a short piece of sashing is sewn to the bottom of each block. The columns are sewn together and then joined with one long piece of sashing. The two side sashing pieces are added and finally the top sashing is attached. The center lift line is moved over to the edge of the center sashing

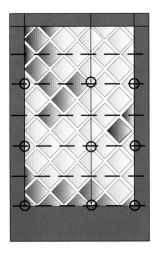

Use short pieces of sashing to create columns. Sew columns together with longer pieces of sashing.

On-point design with sashing.

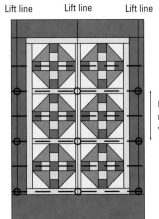

Straight-set design with sashing.

Top Design

A nice look for a Window Hanging is to have a single top row of blocks and then one fabric on the rest of the shade. You lay out the shade as if you were repeating the blocks on the entire inner front so that it folds up correctly. If the bottom portion of the inner front is a single piece of fabric, lay out the piece so that it hangs on the grain. Piecing the lower portion using solid blocks of the background fabric adds interest when the sun shines through. You can also make the shade "borderless" by using the same fabric for the borders as the background, rather than a contrasting fabric. Narrow side and top borders work well with this layout. Allow at least 3/4" side borders so that you can easily sew the side seams. Allow at least a 1" top border for the hook and loop fastener. (Remember that the top border also must be at least as long as the mounting board. Use a projected mount to make this value as small as possible.)

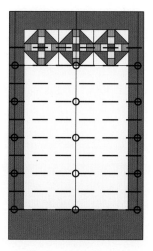

Top design with single piece of fabric.

Top design with pieced bottom portion.

Center Design

With a center design, you lay out the vertical dimension exactly as if you were piecing the entire front. However, when you are laying out the horizontal dimension, you simply center the single column of blocks and then fill in the rest of the width with background fabric and/or side borders. Sketch out your design, drawing in the battens and rings. Make sure that you have seams where you can glue the battens.

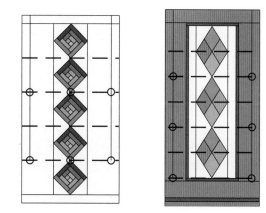

Center design Window Hanging.

Medallions

If you have a square window (or almost square), a medallion quilt looks stunning. Decide upon the approximate size you want for the inner front. Now divide the length of the inner front into equal portions, using the design for guidance. Make sure that your top and bottom borders adhere to the vertical layout rules. If you love math, you will be challenged (and rewarded) by this process. Square the inner front carefully before adding the borders and making the Window Hanging.

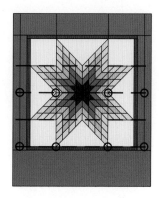

Medallion Window Hanging.

Wall Hangings

The way that we made a Window Hanging out of a pieced front works very well for a wall hanging. Rather than using batting and quilting a wall hanging or stretching it over a frame, follow Steps 1 through 5 on pages 75-79 For wall hangings only, you can use heavy muslin rather than Thermalsuede for the backing. Place a weight rod in the bottom hem of the lining. There is no need to add rings or use pulleys, although you may need to glue a few battens on the inside if the sides sag. Use the smallest piece of wood trim you can find that will accommodate the hook fastener (you can nail right through the fastener). Look at the pine molding display in a lumber store, and choose any appropriate trim piece. If you move, or want a different design on a window, you can convert a Window Hanging to a wall hanging by replacing the mounting board with a small trim piece. When else can you actually use your old window treatments?

Art Quilts

Art quilts are very popular today. Watercolor and Bargello are two techniques that are easy to learn and make wonderful Window Hangings. If you are interested in a particular design, purchase a book describing the technique and carefully study how the geometries are put together. Stay within the constraints given by the author concerning geometry sizes and determine a combination of pieces that you can use as a block height. Once again, if you enjoy the designing aspect of quilting, this will be very satisfying for you.

Reproducing Geometries in Your Room

If you can divide a pattern into squares and triangles, you can piece it. A great custom look is to reproduce a geometry that is already in the room. Wallpaper borders and area rugs provide a wonderful source of inspiration. You will want to choose one part of the design and perhaps simplify it. You can also take part of a pattern that is on a quilt and make a coordinating Window Hanging.

The Possibilities are Endless

I hope that this book has inspired you to adapt your quilting skills to cover your windows. Start out with a simple design. You will quickly move on to more complicated patterns as you realize how satisfying it is to admire your fabric art as functioning shades.

Arts and Crafts in Yellow and Sage,
Terrell Sundermann, 1997.
70" x 58".
Interior design by Steve Neuman.

Photo: Terrell Sundermann

APPENDIX

Shadows Window Hanging Example

This example describes how to lay out and make a Shadows Window Hanging to use as a sample. I urge you to go through the actual math. To make the sample, follow the directions in the blue boxes.

Photo: Steve Vierra

Step 1. Measure Window and Determine Size of Window Hanging

I will use a hybrid mount on this window. My window frame width is 32" wide and 50" long. I want to leave part of the wood showing, so the finished width and length of the Window Hanging will be 30" by 47 1/2".

Since I will need to know the length of the mounting board to lay out the design, I will decide how to mount my shade now. I will use a flat installation, a common pine (1 1/2" x 3/4") wood board and a flat pulley (5/8" long). Also, my lift rings have a diameter of 5/8".

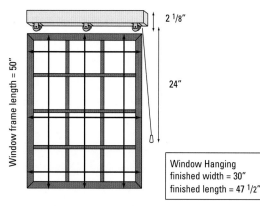

2 1/8"

Window frame length = 50"

24"

Window Hanging
finished width = 30"
finished length = 47 1/2"

Window frame width = 32"

Sketch of window used for Shadows Sample Window Hanging.

Step 2. Plan the Layout

I first must determine the possible block sizes for my quilt block. This is given on page 38. I then use the lay out forms given at the end of this Appendix to design my Window Hanging. I start with the vertical layout process.

Decide upon a half-block fold or a full-block fold. I want a full-block fold so that I can see the entire block when the shade is fully raised. Now I fill out the Full Block Vertical Layout Form.

Vertical a. Determine the smallest top border. The First Vertical Layout Rule is:

Smallest top border = mounting board length + lift ring diameter = 1 1/2" + 5/8" + 5/8" = 2 3/4 "

Vertical b. Choose an initial finished block size. I choose a finished block size of 7 3/4". I highlight this block size from the Shadows Block Size Chart on page 38.

Shadows Block Size Chart

Finished Block Size	Finished Strip Size	Cut Strip Size
6 7/8"	1"	1 1/2"
7 3/4"	1 1/8"	1 5/8"
8 5/8"	1 1/4"	1 3/4"

Vertical c. Determine the smallest bottom border. The Second Vertical Layout Rule for a full block fold is:

$$\text{Smallest bottom border} = \text{block height} + 1"$$
$$= 7\,3/4" + 1" = 8\,3/4"$$

Vertical d. Determine the largest length of the inner front.

$$\text{Largest inner front length} =$$
$$\text{finished length} - \text{smallest top border}$$
$$- \text{smallest bottom border}$$

$$= 47\,1/2" - 2\,3/4" - 8\,3/4" = 36"$$

Vertical e. Determine number of whole blocks that fit into inner front.

Now I determine how many even numbers of blocks I can fit into this inner front length:

$$36" \text{ divided by } 7\,3/4" = 4.6 \text{ blocks}$$

I need to fit a whole even number of blocks into this space, so I round down to 4 blocks.

> **NOTE:** At this point in our layout process, we use an even number of rows when we are folding on the full block. Then at the end of the designing process, we decide whether we will add an additional row of blocks, ending up with an odd number of rows. The half-block fold vertical layout process is easier, since we can have either an odd number or an even number of rows throughout our layout process.

Vertical f. Determine adjusted size of inner front length.

$$\text{Adjusted inner front length} = \text{number of}$$
$$\text{rows} \times \text{block height} = 4 \times 7\,3/4" = 31"$$

Vertical g. Increase the bottom border so that the entire inner front length is filled in. I have a top border of 2 3/4" and my adjusted inner front length is 31", so my adjusted bottom border is:

$$\text{Adjusted bottom border} = \text{finished length} - \text{top}$$
$$\text{border} - \text{adjusted inner front length} =$$

$$47\,1/2" - 2\,3/4" - 31" = 13\,3/4"$$

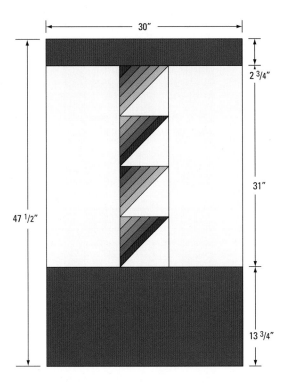

Preliminary sketch after vertical layout process.

Full-Block Vertical Layout Form

(See page 57 for step by step instructions)

Repeat process as needed

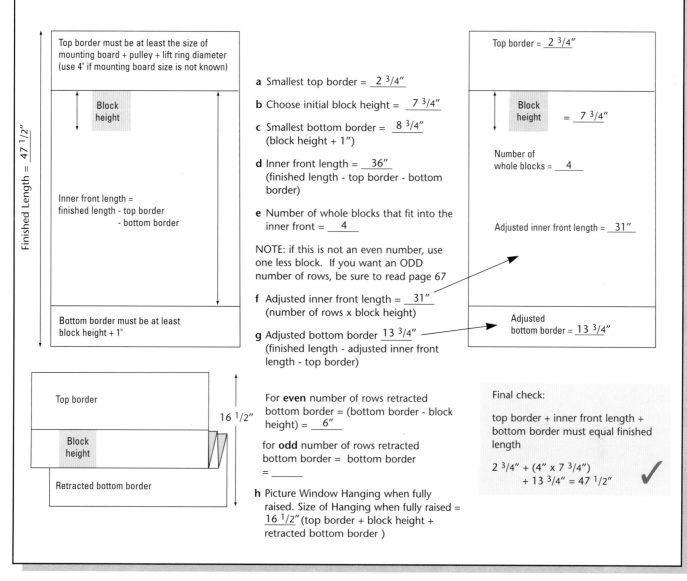

Finished Length = 47 1/2"

Top border must be at least the size of mounting board + pulley + lift ring diameter (use 4" if mounting board size is not known)

Block height

Inner front length = finished length - top border - bottom border

Bottom border must be at least block height + 1"

a Smallest top border = __2 3/4"__

b Choose initial block height = __7 3/4"__

c Smallest bottom border = __8 3/4"__ (block height + 1")

d Inner front length = __36"__ (finished length - top border - bottom border)

e Number of whole blocks that fit into the inner front = __4__

NOTE: if this is not an even number, use one less block. If you want an ODD number of rows, be sure to read page 67

f Adjusted inner front length = __31"__ (number of rows x block height)

g Adjusted bottom border __13 3/4"__ (finished length - adjusted inner front length - top border)

Top border = __2 3/4"__

Block height = __7 3/4"__

Number of whole blocks = __4__

Adjusted inner front length = __31"__

Adjusted bottom border = __13 3/4"__

Top border

Block height

Retracted bottom border

16 1/2"

For **even** number of rows retracted bottom border = (bottom border - block height) = __6"__

for **odd** number of rows retracted bottom border = bottom border = _____

h Picture Window Hanging when fully raised. Size of Hanging when fully raised = __16 1/2"__ (top border + block height + retracted bottom border)

Final check:

top border + inner front length + bottom border must equal finished length

2 3/4" + (4" x 7 3/4") + 13 3/4" = 47 1/2" ✓

To determine the side borders I use the Horizontal Layout Form.

Horizontal a. My block width is 7 3/4", the same as the block height.

Horizontal b. Choose an initial side border width. I will start with a side border of 3".

Horizontal c. Determine the initial inner front width.

Inner front width =
finished width - 2 x side border widths
= 30" - (2 x 3") = 24"

Horizontal d. Place as many blocks as possible across this width.

Number of blocks =
inner front divided by block size
= 24" divided by 7 3/4" = 3.1 blocks
(Round down to (3) three blocks)

Horizontal e. Determine the adjusted inner front width.

Adjusted inner front width =
number of blocks across x block width
= 3 x 7 3/4" = 23 1/4"

Widen or narrow the side borders to fill the entire front. I will widen the borders so that I have three columns of blocks. My adjusted side borders will be determined by the adjusted inner front width:

Side border =
(finished width – inner front width)/2
= (30 - 23 1/4")/2
= 6 3/4" / 2 = 3 3/8"

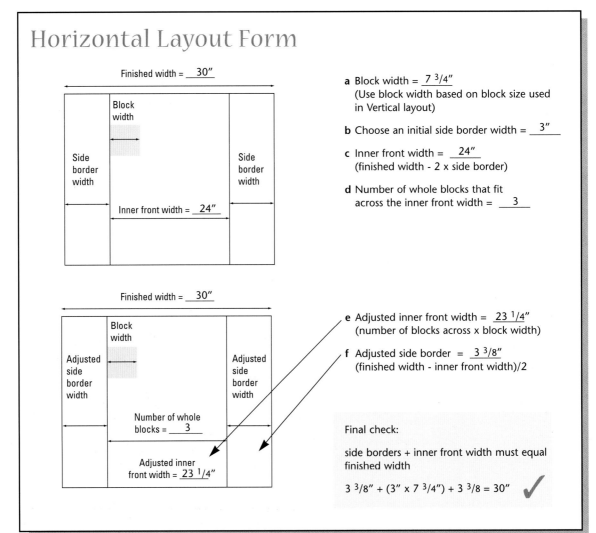

Horizontal Layout Form

Finished width = __30"__

Block width

Side border width

Side border width

Inner front width = __24"__

a Block width = __7 3/4"__
(Use block width based on block size used in Vertical layout)

b Choose an initial side border width = __3"__

c Inner front width = __24"__
(finished width - 2 x side border)

d Number of whole blocks that fit across the inner front width = __3__

Finished width = __30"__

Block width

Adjusted side border width

Adjusted side border width

Number of whole blocks = __3__

Adjusted inner front = __23 1/4"__

e Adjusted inner front width = __23 1/4"__
(number of blocks across x block width)

f Adjusted side border = __3 3/8"__
(finished width - inner front width)/2

Final check:

side borders + inner front width must equal finished width

3 3/8" + (3" x 7 3/4") + 3 3/8 = 30" ✓

I now adjust my top and bottom borders, keeping the total border length constant:

Total border length = top border + bottom border
= 2 3/4" + 13 3/4" = 16 1/2".

Since my side borders are 3 3/8", I will increase the top border to 3 3/4". This means that the bottom border is:

Bottom border = total border length – top border
= 16 1/2" - 3 3/4" = 12 3/4".

I still have a very long bottom border, so I will add a row of blocks at the bottom. Up to this point, I had an even number of rows. Since my block is 7 3/4" long, I can place a row on top of my 12 3/4" bottom border. This means that my new bottom border is:

New bottom border (odd number of rows) = old bottom border (even number of rows) - block height
= 12 3/4" - 7 3/4" = 5"

Step 3. Sketch Your Final Drawing

My final drawing is shown with batten locations and the folds are marked. Notice that since I have an odd number of rows, my lowest batten (and first row of lift rings) is placed at the bottom of the **second** row of blocks. The lowest row of blocks will fold up behind the shade when it is raised. The Shadows block A and Shadows block B are also labeled. I have a total of eight A-blocks and seven B-blocks. I will use three lift lines, one on each edge of the shade and one in the center. I mark the lift ring locations (on each up fold) on the drawing.

The most important thing that I can do now is to add up all of my numbers and check the two Vertical Layout Rules. This is the only way that I can be sure that my shade will fold up correctly (other than cutting out the drawing and folding the paper, which works very well).

Finished length = 3 3/4"(top border) + 7 3/4"+ 7 3/4"+ 7 3/4"+ 7 3/4"+ 7 3/4"(5 rows of blocks) + 5"(bottom border) = 47 1/2" (finished length)

Finished width = 3 3/8"(side border) + 7 3/4"+ 7 3/4"+ 7 3/4"(3 columns of blocks) + 3 3/8" (side border) = 30" (finished width)

First Vertical Layout Rule: Top border must be greater than 2 3/4" (it is 3 3/4").

Second Vertical Layout Rule: Bottom border must be greater than 1" for an odd number of rows, full-fold design (it is 5").

Check the retracted border: this is the same as our bottom border, in the case of an odd number of rows, full-fold design. The fully raised drawing shows how the shade will look when up.

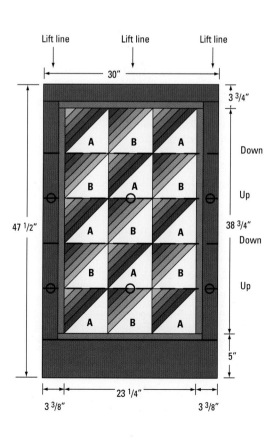

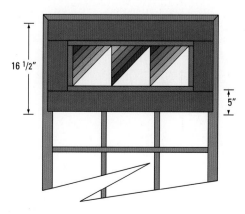

Step 4. Determine Your Fabric Requirements for the Blocks

I use the Fabric Requirements Charts for the Shadows block given on page 39 to determine the yardage for the blocks. I have 8 A blocks and 7 B blocks. I can get up to 10 A blocks (finished block size of 7 $3/4$") and 10 B blocks from $1/4$ yard of each fabric. This allows two extra blocks of each type.

Fabric Requirements for Colored Strip Sets

Finished Block Size	Size of Cut Strip	Number of blocks you can make from $1/4$ yard of each fabric
6"	1 $3/8$"	18 A blocks and 18 B Blocks
6 $7/8$"	1 $1/2$"	18 A blocks and 18 B Blocks
7 $3/4$"	1 $5/8$"	10 A blocks and 10 B Blocks
8 $5/8$"	1 $3/4$"	10 A blocks and 10 B Blocks
9 $1/2$"	1 $7/8$"	8 A blocks and 8 B Blocks

I need 15 solid triangles (8 + 7). I can get 16 triangles from $1/2$ yard of fabric. This leaves me only one triangle over what I need, so I want to buy extra yardage in case I goof. I see that my triangles are going to be cut from 8 $5/8$" squares, so I need to get another $1/4$ yard, for a total of $3/4$ yard.

Fabric Requirements for Solid Triangles

Finished Block Size	Cut Size of for Block Half Square Triangle	Number of Triangles you can get from 1/2 yd of fabric
6"	6 $7/8$"	20
6 $7/8$"	7 $3/4$"	20
7 $3/4$"	8 $5/8$"	16
8 $5/8$"	9 $1/2$"	8
9 $1/2$"	10 $3/8$"	6

Step 5. Determine Your Fabric Requirements for the Borders

Using the instructions on page 69 and the sketch of the Window Hanging, I can determine the cut sizes of my border pieces (I will be using a $3/4$" accent border):

Cut two (2) side borders

Cut width = side border + 3 $1/4$" =
3 $3/8$ " + 3 1/4" = 6 $5/8$"

Cut length = inner length + 6" =
38 $3/4$" + 6" = 44 $3/4$"

Cut one (1) top border

Cut width = top border length + 3 $1/4$ " =
3 $3/4$" + 3 $1/4$" = 7"

Cut length = finished width + 5" =
30" + 5" = 35"

Cut one (1) bottom border

Cut width = bottom border length
- accent border finished width + 6 $1/4$" =

5" - $3/4$" + 6 $1/4$" = 10 $1/2$"

Cut length = finished width + 5" =
30" + 5" = 35"

I sketch out my border pieces and determine that I can use one fabric width for all four of my border pieces, and I need 44 $3/4$", which is 1.24 yards. I will purchase an extra $1/4$ yard to allow for errors. So the total yardage I need for the borders is 1 $1/2$ yards.

The accent border pieces will be cut in strips that are $3/4$" + $1/2$" = 1 $1/4$":

Cut length for sides = inner length +3" =
38 $3/4$"+ 3" = 41 $3/4$" (cut two)

Cut length for top and bottom =
inner width + 4" =
23 $1/4$" + 4" = 27 $1/4$" (cut two)

Looking at the strip lengths above, I will buy half a yard extra of the accent border fabric (it is also used in the block) cut vertical strips and then piece them into the correct sizes.

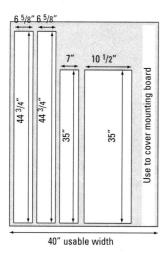

6 5/8" 6 5/8"

7" 10 1/2"

44 3/4" 44 3/4" 35" 35"

Use to cover mounting board

40" usable width

Sketch of border pieces.

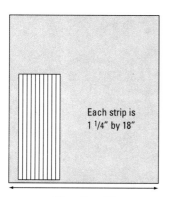

Each strip is 1 1/4" by 18"

40" usable width

Sketch of accent border pieces.

Step 6. Determine Your Lining Requirements

I use the directions on page 71 to determine the amount of lining needed and to sketch a cutting diagram.

$$\text{Cut lining length} = \text{finished length} + 12"$$
$$= 47 \, 1/2" + 12" = 59 \, 1/2"$$

$$\text{Cut lining width} = \text{finished width} + 3"$$
$$= 30" + 3" = 33"$$

I will need to purchase 59 1/2" of lining, which is 1.65 yards. I can round up to the nearest 1/8 yard (the calculation already adds extra inches for me) and purchase 1 3/4 yards of 48" wide lining.

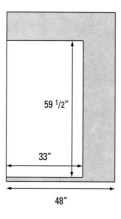

59 1/2"

33"

48"

Sketch of lining.

You'll Need:

1/4 yard blue fabric for stripe **a** plus another 1 1/2 yards for borders

1/4 yard dark teal fabric for stripe **b**

1/4 yard medium dark teal fabric for stripe **c** plus another 1/2 yard for accent border

1/4 yard medium light teal fabric for stripe **d**

1/4 yard light teal fabric for stripe **e**

3/4 yard cream fabric for triangle blocks

1 3/4 yards of 48" wide Roc-Lon Thermalsuede lining

Step 7. Determine Your Hardware Requirements.

I used the instructions on page 106 to determine my hardware requirements:

Hook and loop fastener:
length = finished width + 2" = 30" + 2" = 32"

Battens:
length = finished width + 1" = 30" + 1" = 31"

Number of battens =
4 (I counted these on my drawing)

Number of lift rings =
6 (I counted these on my drawing)

Number of pulleys = number of lift lines = 3

Lift cord length =
number of lift lines x (2 x finished length + finished width)

$$= 3 \times (2 \times 47 \tfrac{1}{2}" + 30)"$$
$$= 3 \times 125" = 375" = 10.4 \text{ yards}$$

Weight rod length = finished width + 1" = 30" + 1" = 31"

Mounting board = finished width + 1" = 30" + 1" = 31"

Fabric to cover mounting board use remnants from fabric *b*

One cord drop and cleat

Step 8 through Step 10. Making the Window Hanging

Make the shade using the instructions given in Project 1, pages 40 - 41.

Cutting

From each $1/4$ yard of the blue, dark teal, medium dark teal, medium light teal, and light teal fabrics, cut:

    5 (1 $5/8$"- wide) strips

From cream fabric, cut:

    2 (8 $5/8$"- wide) strips. From these, cut 8 (8 $5/8$" x 8 $5/8$") squares. Cut each square diagonally into two triangles

From the extra $1/2$ yard piece of medium dark teal fabric, cut:

    10 (1 $1/4$" x 18") pieces

From the 1 $1/2$ yard piece of blue fabric, cut (use the border fabric drawing):

    2 (6 $5/8$" x 44 $3/4$") rectangles, 1 (7" x 35") rectangle, 1 (10 $1/2$" x 35") rectangle

Thoroughly steam press and then cut the lining fabric:

    1 (33" x 59 $1/2$") rectangle

Sewing the Blocks

Lay out your strips into color sets: blue, dark teal, medium dark teal, medium light teal, and light teal. Your will have five sets. Sew the strips together. Press seams in one direction. Use the directions on page 41 to make a template to cut the triangles. Our finished block size is 7 $3/4$" and the template's triangle height is 6 $1/8$". (Shortcut: use the extra cream triangle to make a template.)

Refer to the Illustration on page 41 to cut 8 A-triangles and 7 B-triangles. Sew the solid triangles to your striped triangles along the diagonal and press seam towards the pieced section. Continue with the directions in Project 1, page 41 to complete your shade.

Special Notes

Sew the accent border pieces into one long strip. Then cut into lengths for the sides, top and bottom of your inner front.

After sewing on the borders, trim the sides of your pieced front so that you have a raw-edge to raw-edge width of 32".

Fold the top of the front so that the finished length is 47 $1/2$". Trim $3/4$" above the fold line and attach loop fastener so that it overlaps the raw edges.

Measure your complete Window Hanging. It should be 30" wide and 47 $1/2$" long. If so, then you can cut your hardware as follows: (If you end up with a shade that is not 30" wide, follow directions from the Hardware Worksheet on page 106 to adjust your hardware cutting measurements.)

    Cut 4 battens (29 $1/2$")

    Cut wooden board (29 $3/4$")

    Cut border remnant (35" x 5 $1/2$") to cover board

    Cut steel rod (29")

Glue the lowest batten along the bottom of the *second* row of blocks. Refer to the drawing showing the batten locations.

To operate your sample Window Hanging, attach the mounting board to the top of the shade, string the lift cords as described on page 83. Braid the cords and attach the cord drop. You can hold the mounting board in one hand and raise and lower the shade with the other hand.

Full-Block Vertical Layout Form

(See page 57 for step by step instructions)

Repeat process as needed

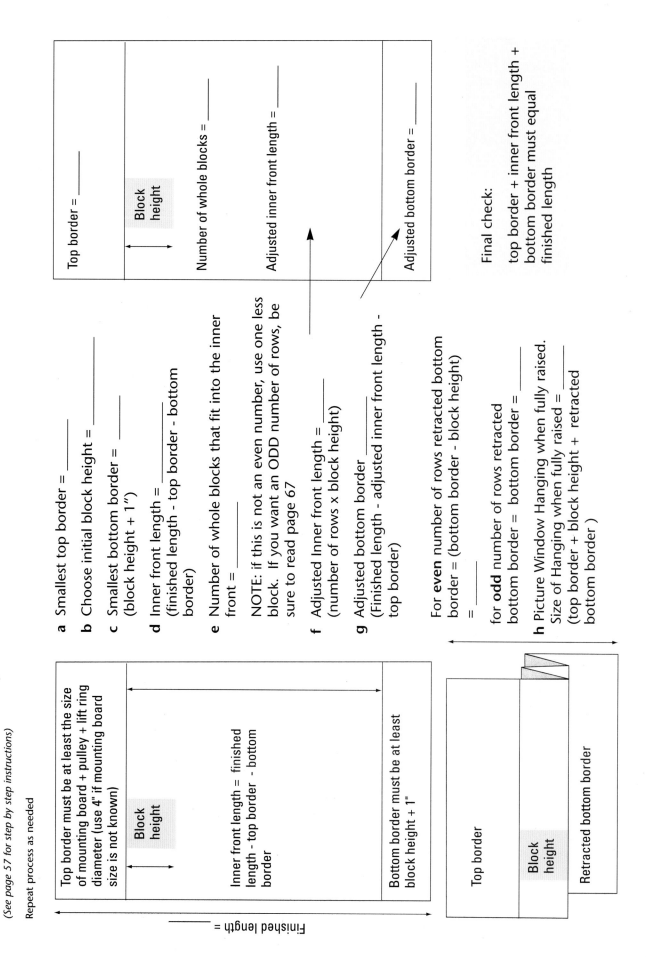

a Smallest top border = _____

b Choose initial block height = _____

c Smallest bottom border = _____
(block height + 1")

d Inner front length = _____
(finished length - top border - bottom border)

e Number of whole blocks that fit into the inner front = _____

NOTE: if this is not an even number, use one less block. If you want an ODD number of rows, be sure to read page 67

f Adjusted Inner front length = _____
(number of rows x block height)

g Adjusted bottom border _____
(Finished length - adjusted inner front length - top border)

For **even** number of rows retracted bottom border = (bottom border - block height)
= _____

for **odd** number of rows retracted bottom border = bottom border = _____

h Picture Window Hanging when fully raised. Size of Hanging when fully raised = _____
(top border + block height + retracted bottom border)

Final check:

top border + inner front length + bottom border must equal finished length

Top border = _____

Block height

Number of whole blocks = _____

Adjusted inner front length = _____

Adjusted bottom border = _____

Top border must be at least the size of mounting board + pulley + lift ring diameter (use 4" if mounting board size is not known)

Block height

Inner front length = finished length - top border - bottom border

Bottom border must be at least block height + 1"

Finished length = _____

Top border

Block height

Retracted bottom border

Half-Block Vertical Layout Form

(See page 57 for step by step instructions)

Repeat process as needed

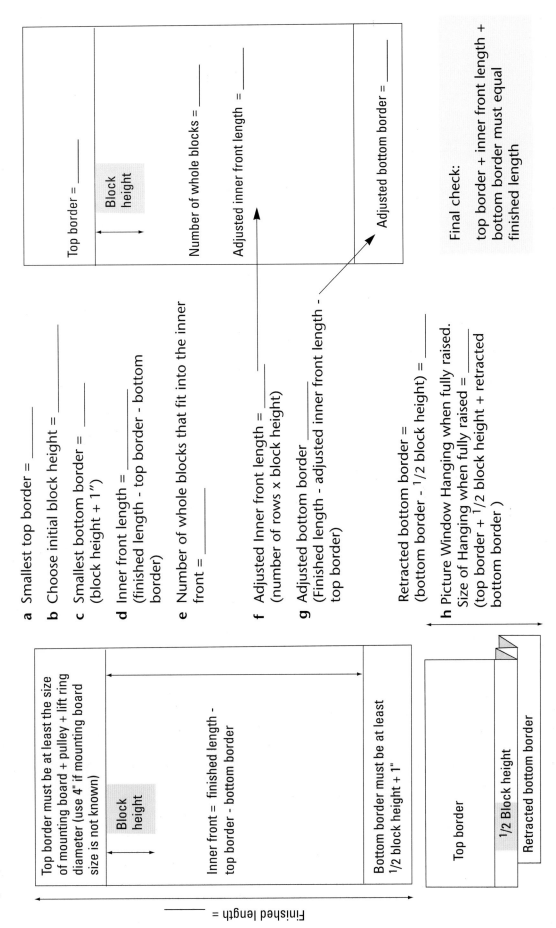

a Smallest top border = _____

b Choose initial block height = _____

c Smallest bottom border = _____
(block height + 1")

d Inner front length = _____
(finished length - top border - bottom border)

e Number of whole blocks that fit into the inner front = _____

f Adjusted Inner front length = _____
(number of rows x block height)

g Adjusted bottom border _____
(Finished length - adjusted inner front length - top border)

Retracted bottom border = _____
(bottom border - ¹/2 block height) = _____

h Picture Window Hanging when fully raised.
Size of Hanging when fully raised = _____
(top border + ¹/2 block height + retracted bottom border)

Final check:

top border + inner front length + bottom border must equal finished length

Top border = _____

Block height

Number of whole blocks = _____

Adjusted inner front length = _____

Adjusted bottom border = _____

Top border must be at least the size of mounting board + pulley + lift ring diameter (use 4" if mounting board size is not known)

Block height

Inner front = finished length - top border - bottom border

Bottom border must be at least ¹/2 block height + 1"

Finished length = _____

Top border

¹/2 Block height

Retracted bottom border

Horizontal Layout Form

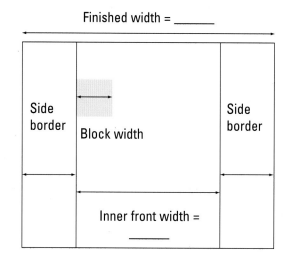

Finished width = _____

Side border

Block width

Side border

Inner front width = _____

a Block width = _____
Use block width based on block size used in Vertical layout a

b Choose an initial side border = _____

c Inner front width = _____
(finished width - 2 x side border)

d Number of whole blocks that fit across the inner front width = _____

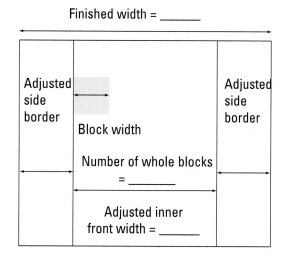

Finished width = _____

Adjusted side border

Block width

Number of whole blocks = _____

Adjusted inner front width = _____

Adjusted side border

e Adjusted inner front width = _____
(number of blocks across x block width)

f Adjusted side border = _____
(finished width - inner front width)/2

Final check: side borders + inner front width must equal finished width

Window Measurement Form

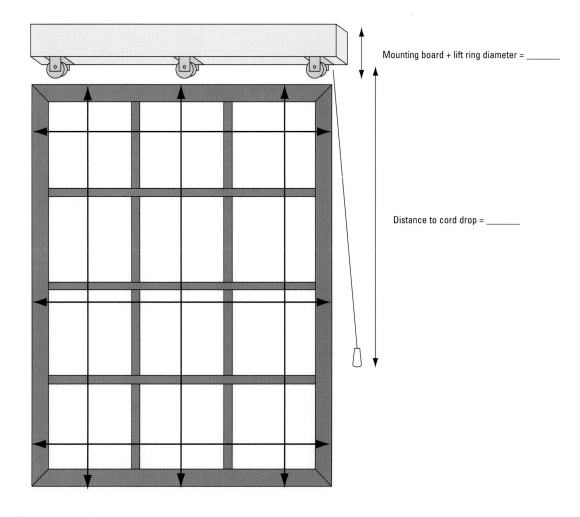

Mounting board + lift ring diameter = _____

Distance to cord drop = _____

Measure your window in three places both horizontally and vertically.

Hardware Worksheet and Shopping List

Item	Amount to Buy	Finished Size	I Need
Mounting Board	Add 1" to the finished width of the Window Hanging	Length: Cut $1/4$" less than width of Window Hanging at top	Length:
Fabric to cover mounting board	Calculate: Length: Add 5" to the length of mounting board Width: Add $3/4$" to the circumference of the mounting board	Trim as needed while covering mounting board	Length: Width:
Hook and loop fastener	Add 2 " to the finished width of Window Hanging	Trim to fit after attaching to Window Hanging and mounting board	Length:
Battens	Length: Add 1" to the finished width of Window Hanging Number: 1 batten for each fold	Length: Cut to $1/2$" less than finished width of Window Hanging	Length: Number:
Weight rod	Length: Add 1" to the finished width of the Window Hanging Number: 1 per Window Hanging	Length: Cut to $1/2$" less than finished width of **lining** at hem	Length: Number:
Lift rings	Count or calculate (number of up folds) x (number of lift lines)		Number:
Pulleys	1 pulley for each lift line		Number:
Lift cord	To calculate the amount of lift cord needed: Multiply the finished length of the Window Hanging by 2, then add the finished width of the Window Hanging. Multiply this number by the number of lift lines.	Trim after rigging	Length:
Cord drop and cleat	1 each per Window Hanging		Number:

Fabric Shopping List

Fabric	Description/Color	I Need (yards)
Fabric 1		
Fabric 2		
Fabric 3		
Fabric 4		
Fabric 5		
Fabric 6		
Fabric 7		
Fabric 8		
Fabric 9		
Background fabric		
Border fabric		
Accent border fabric		
Lining fabric		

Supply List

Item	Description/Color	I Need
Sewing Thread		
Heavy duty thread (match fabric at lift ring locations)		
Glue to attach battens (Gem-Tac or Jewel-It)		
Fabric Protectant (Scotchgard or Quiltgard)		

Illusions Triangle Chart

	Number of Normal Triangles	Number of Reversed Triangles	Total Number of Triangles
Light 1			
Light 2			
Medium 1			
Medium 2			
Medium 3			
Dark 1			
Dark 2			
Dark 3			

Illusions Valance Triangle Chart

	Number of Normal Triangles	Number of Reversed Triangles	Total
Light 1			
Light 2			
Light 3			
Medium 1			
Medium 2			
Medium 3			
Dark 1			
Dark 2			
Dark 3			

INDEX

RESOURCES

Quilting Books

Edie, Marge. *Bargello Quilts*
Bothell, WA: That Patchwork Place, 1994

Fons, Marianne, and Porter, Liz. *Quilter's Complete Guide*
Birmingham, AL: Oxmoor House, 1993.

Martin, Judy. *The Block Book*
Grinnell, IA: Crosley-Griffith Publishing Company, 1998

McClun, Diana and Laura Nownes. *Quilts, Quilts and More Quilts*
Concord, CA: C&T Publishing, 1993

Perry, Gai. *Impressionist Quilts*
Lafayette, CA: C&T Publishing, 1995

Perry, Gai. *Impressionist Palette*
Concord, CA: C&T Publishing, 1998

Window Treatment Books

Curtains, Draperies & Shades
Menlo Park, CA: Sunset Books, 1993

Sewing for the Home, Singer Sewing
Reference Library
Minnetonka, MI: Cowles Creative Publishing, 1995

Lining Sources

General fabric stores that carry decorator fabrics will have a variety of drapery linings. Be sure that you use a lining that blocks ultraviolet light.

Roman Shade Hardware Sources

Hardware for making shades and valances out of your fabric art may be obtained from your local hardware store or home sewing store.

Terrell Designs
5325 Sanford Circle East
Englewood, CO 80110
303-639-9876
E-mail: terrelldesigns@prodigy.net

Mail order for all required hardware to make Window Hangings. Services offered are design review of your layout and making your pieced front into a shade.

Tool Sources

You can purchase carpenter's squares and aluminum rulers in your hardware and home supply store.

Atlanta-National Thread & Supply
695 Red Oak Road
Stockbridge, GA 30281
777-389-9115
800-331-7600
FAX: 800-298-0403
aluminum rulers (48", 60" and 72")

Wholesale Sources

Retail quilt fabric stores should check their Yellow Pages for local wholesale sources of drapery lining and drapery hardware. Mail order wholesale suppliers of all necessary parts are listed below. Many have a low minimum order ($15.00 in some cases) and will take credit cards over the telephone. You must be an established business with a valid resale license to purchase through these sources.

Dofix No Sew, Inc.
1947 Ironway Drive
Sanford, MI 48657
517-687-7999
800-962-8983
FAX: 517-687-7220
soft sew-on loop and hook fastener
(Don't purchase their plastic rollers in place of pulleys, they are not strong enough for fabric shades.)

Kirsch
309 N. Prospect
Sturgis, MI 49091
616-659-5100
FAX: 800-760-0033
solid pulleys, cord cleats, weighted cord drops
This manufacturer can also supply you with a local distributor who stocks their products.

Rockland Mills
P. O. Box 17293
Baltimore, MD 21203
410-522-2505
800-876-2566
FAX: 410-522-2545
Roc-lon Thermalsuede drapery lining
This manufacturer can supply you with a local distributor who stocks their products.

Rowley Company
230 Meek Road
P. O. Box 6010
Gastonia, NC 28056
704-866-0650
800-343-4542
FAX: 704-868-9787
FAX: 800-554-0407

Roman shade ribs, rib splices, steel rodding, lift cord, lift rings, cord cleats, rulers (48", 60", 72" and 96").
This mail order wholesale supplier carries a wide line of drapery workroom supplies and tools. Don't use their sew-on loop fastener, it is too stiff. Also, don't use their unweighted cord drops, which are flimsy. This is the only known supplier of the Roman shade ribs.

Silverado Service Company
2130 Pickett Road
Calistoga, CA 94515
707-942-5800
FAX: 707-942-5624
flat pulleys, cord cleats, lift cord, lift rings.

About the AUTHOR

Terrell Sundermann grew up in southwestern Kansas and was taught to sew in early childhood by her grandmother. Terrell received a Ph.D. in Physics from the University of Illinois in 1979 and enjoyed gaining experience in manufacturing and technical marketing in several electronics companies in the Boston area. However, her love (and escape) was always making beautiful things with her hands. Terrell is a "self-taught" sewer, and tends to see a picture in a book and then "just make it". She has an innate eye for color and fabric combinations. After making a log cabin wall hanging, Terrell began experimenting with combining a wall hanging and a Roman shade. Her background in physics proved valuable as she perfected the functional portion of Window Hangings.

When a successful career in high-tech manufacturing failed to fulfill her creative needs, Terrell left the corporate world and founded Terrell Designs in 1993. She now designs and fabricates custom fabric art for window and walls. Terrell Designs' clients include interior designers and homeowners. In addition to Window Hangings, Terrell designs valances, wall hangings and accessories such as pillows and place mats.

Terrell's beautiful shades have been featured in Show Homes in Colorado and Massachusetts and are installed in homes throughout the United

States. It was during one of these exhibits that Terrell noticed the reaction of quilters to her invention. A home sewer would rush up to a shade, look at the back, pull it up and down, stand back and admire it. Then she would return with a notebook (and perhaps a fellow stitcher) and attempt to figure out how to make one for herself. This book is an acknowledgement of that interest and a desire to share years of experience with quilting enthusiasts.

Terrell lives in Cherry Hills Village, Colorado with her husband Ned, where they enjoy all aspects of living in Colorado: skiing, hiking, bicycling and gardening. If you are interested in Terrell's lectures or workshops on designing Window Hangings, write her at 5325 Sanford Circle East, Cherry Hills Village, CO 80110-5107. Terrell also will review your Window Hanging designs and make your front into a shade.

Other Fine Books From C&T Publishing

The Art of Classic Quiltmaking, Harriet Hargrave and Sharyn Craig

At Home with Patrick Lose: Colorful Quilted Projects, Patrick Lose

Color From the Heart: Seven Great Ways to Make Quilts with Colors You Love, Gai Perry

Curves in Motion: Quilt Designs & Techniques, Judy B. Dales

Exploring Machine Trapunto: New Dimensions, Hari Walner

Fabric Shopping with Alex Anderson, Seven Project to Help You: Make, Successful Choices, Build Your Confidence, Add to Your Fabric Stash, Alex Anderson

Faces & Places: Images in Appliqué, Charlotte Warr Andersen

Fantastic Fabric Folding: Innovative Quilting Projects, Rebecca Wat

Focus on Features: Life-like Portrayals in Appliqué, Charlotte Warr Andersen

Freddy's House: Brilliant Color in Quilts, Freddy Moran

Free Stuff for Collectors on the Internet, Judy Heim and Gloria Hansen

Free Stuff for Crafty Kids on the Internet, Judy Heim and Gloria Hansen

Free Stuff for Gardeners on the Internet, Judy Heim and Gloria Hansen

Free Stuff for Quilters on the Internet, 2nd Ed., Judy Heim and Gloria Hansen

Free Stuff for Sewing Fanatics on the Internet, Judy Heim and Gloria Hansen

Free Stuff for Stitchers on the Internet, Judy Heim and Gloria Hansen

Hand Quilting with Alex Anderson: Six Projects for Hand Quilters, Alex Anderson

Heirloom Machine Quilting, Third Edition, Harriet Hargrave

Jacobean Rhapsodies: Composing with 28 Appliqué Designs, Patricia B. Campbell and Mimi Ayars

Mastering Machine Appliqué, Harriet Hargrave

Mastering Quilt Marking: Marking Tools & Techniques, Choosing Stencils, Matching Borders & Corners, Pepper Cory

The New England Quilt Museum Quilts: Featuring the Story of the Mill Girls. With Instructions for 5 Heirloom Quilts, Jennifer Gilbert

The Photo Transfer Handbook: Snap It, Print It, Stitch It!, Jean Ray Laury

Pieced Flowers, Ruth B. McDowell

Piecing: Expanding the Basics, Ruth B. McDowell

Quilts from Europe, Projects and Inspiration, Gül Laporte

Quilts from the Civil War: Nine Projects, Historical Notes, Diary Entries, Barbara Brackman

Rotary Cutting with Alex Anderson: Tips, Techniques, and Projects, Alex Anderson

Rx for Quilters: Stitcher-Friendly Advice for Every Body, Susan Delaney Mech, M.D.

Shadow Quilts: Easy-to-Design Multiple Image Quilts, Patricia Maxiner Magaret and Donna Ingram Slusser

Skydyes: A Visual Guide to Fabric Painting, Mickey Lawler

Special Delivery Quilts, Patrick Lose

Start Quilting with Alex Anderson: Six Projects for First-Time Quilters, Alex Anderson

Through the Garden Gate: Quilters and Their Gardens, Jean and Valori Wells

Travels with Peaky and Spike: Doreen Speckmann's Quilting Adventures, Doreen Speckmann

Wild Birds: Designs for Appliqué & Quilting, Carol Armstrong

Wildflowers: Designs for Appliqué & Quilting, Carol Armstrong

Women of Taste: A Collaboration Celebrating Quilt Artists and Chefs, Girls, Inc.

For more information write for a free catalog:

C&T Publishing, Inc.
P.O. Box 1456
Lafayette, CA 94549
(800) 284-1114
http://www.ctpub.com
e-mail: ctinfo@ctpub.com

For quilting supplies:
Cotton Patch Mail Order
3405 Hall Lane, Dept. CTB
Lafayette, CA 94549
e-mail: quiltusa@yahoo.com
web: www.quiltusa.com
(800) 835-4418
(925) 283-7883